Witnesses of the Way

Witnesses of the Way

The Interior Life
of Some Famous Christians

by

George Allen Turner

BEACON HILL PRESS OF KANSAS CITY
Kansas City, Missouri

Copyright, 1981
Beacon Hill Press of Kansas City

ISBN: 0-8341-0692-2

Printed in the
United States of America

Contents

Foreword

Personal accounts of how God's promises of victory over sin have become reality in human experience stretch across the entire span of Christian history. Such witnesses confirm the nature and truth of God's grace in Jesus Christ at work in the hearts of His people. The firm witness of believers' personal wholeness in Christ and victory over sin has encouraged and challenged other Christians to persevere and realize new depths of grace.

In spite of the traditionalism with which the accounts are often overladen, the spiritual achievements of medieval saints such as Francis of Assisi and Thomas a Kempis still challenge us to lives of holiness. Out of the Wesley-Evangelical revival, when the teaching of the possibilities of holiness in Christian experience was renewed, testimonies to the present reality of the truth flourished anew. John Fletcher, Hester Ann Rogers, Elizabeth Fry, and a host of lesser known believers told of the fullness of salvation they had found by faith and complete surrender to God.

Their experiences in turn fed the fires of the holiness-deeper life revivals in 19th-century America. Again numerous collections of personal experiences of entire sanctification or the baptism or fullness of the Spirit appeared. Such works as Phoebe Palmer's *Pioneer Experiences* urged men and women everywhere to go on to perfection in love. In our own century the Christian experience and understanding of Oswald Chambers and Lettie Cowman led thousands of believers toward total commitment and new spiritual victory as they read the devotional writings of these vibrant Christians.

Dr. Turner has gathered together in this volume many witnesses to Christian experience whose testimonies follow similar men and women in a long tradition in the history of Christianity. In the darkest hour of spiritual despair or in the moment of supreme satisfaction their lives call us from "mere Christianity" to fullness of faith and total surrender.

All these testify that true Christianity is always translatable into life—that life "in Christ" is "the way" of realization and full salvation. The "redeemed of the Lord" do indeed say so in these pages. To the person who is seeking, they say, "The view from the heights is as beautiful as is promised; we have been there. The dark valley is never without a light, and we have walked there. Come follow Christ with us and you, too, will know His Word is true."

These witnesses tell of God's goodness and blessing, not their own virtue or accomplishments. But the searching soul hears them and says, "The promises of life in the Spirit are true. I can realize them today in faith and obedience. They have been known by these and they can be real to me." In these pages truth becomes life; we can see it. Faith is renewed; the hope of "full salvation" and of "love made perfect" is transformed into reality. In our own way, in our own experience we, too, can believe for the fullness of life promised to every child of God through Jesus Christ and the sanctifying Spirit.

M. E. DIETER
Associate Professor of Church History
Asbury Theological Seminary
Wilmore, Ky.

Preface

Across the centuries one may detect a continuity of witness to the possibilities of divine grace in the lives of men and women. Here is a gallery of 100 witnesses from many continents and walks of life; they share their experience of the work of Christ in their lives. Their testimonies are stimulating, refreshing and challenging to all interested in vital Christian living. In recent years personal testimonies have been received with greater respect than formerly, due in part to the influence of existentialism. There is a new appreciation for sincerity and authenticity.

Common to each of these witnesses is progress *after* their reception of the divine life in regeneration. Their language varies greatly as may be expected. But the variety, with no stereotyped phraseology, lends to the inner core of the truth to which they bear witness. Some are famous, others are not. These witnesses are selected on the basis of the note of authenticity of which they report the grace of God experienced.

These witnesses provide convincing evidence that those (including reborn Christians) "who hunger and thirst after righteousness" may be filled and fulfilled. These have *obtained* (not attained) what may be called Christian perfection, perfect love, entire sanctification, the fullness of the Holy Spirit—terms emerging from the language of Scripture and formalized in historical theology. Because these witness to divine grace *obtained* as a gift, not *attained* as a reward, it is appropriate that they share their experience to the glory of God and not for self-

11

aggrandizement. There is consequently no grounds for boasting except in the Pauline sense of glorying in God's grace received through Christ.

In Pietism the stress is on the individual's experience of divine grace; in Anabaptist tradition the stress is on discipleship, on service. Both are equally essential. Because experience is stressed in these pages, it is not to be assumed that subsequent growth, progress, and service to others is less important. The focus on experience in this volume seems justified because a "crisis experience" following conversion is seen as basic to further growth and also because it is a factor too often neglected.

These witnesses are from a variety of backgrounds but share in common new life in Christ. Because of the fact that they are human and share Christ, they speak to us—if we will listen.

GEORGE ALLEN TURNER
Asbury Theological Seminary

Introduction

The earliest name for the Christian movement was simply "the way." Believers were designated as "any of *this way*" (Acts 9:2; this page's emphases added). Later, at the important city of Ephesus, "there arose no small stir about *that way*" (Acts 19:23; cf. v. 9). Paul is quoted as saying that he "persecuted *this way*," and that the governor Felix had "more perfect knowledge of *that way*" (Acts 22:4; 24:22; cf. v. 14). The term "Christian" is found only three times in the New Testament (Acts 11:26; 26:28; 1 Pet. 4:16) and used only by outsiders looking at those of "the way."

The analogy of a path or road is rather prominent in both Old and New Testaments. In the Old Testament God's will is called "the *way* of truth" (Ps. 119:30), and also the Psalmist declares that God's "*way* is perfect" (Ps. 18:30). A well-known passage describes "The *way* of holiness" (Isa. 35:8). Both Old and New Testaments contain admonitions to "walk with the Lord" in this "*way*." Enoch, Noah, and Abraham "walked" with the Lord. Certain of the Hebrew kings sought "to walk in all his ways" (1 Kings 8:58; cf. 2 Chron. 17:3-4).

Jesus exhorted His hearers to enter in "at the strait gate" which leads to life (Matt. 7:13-14). Discipleship consisted of "walking" with Jesus; and when some defected, they were said to have "walked no more with him" (John 6:66). Believers are urged to "walk in the light, as he is in the light" as the condition of fellowship and purity (1 John 1:7). In addition, Paul spoke of a "more excellent

13

way" which he proceeded to describe in terms which constitute one of the most beloved chapters of the New Testament (1 Corinthians 13). This "more excellent way" Paul defined as the way of faith, hope, and love. All of this is one of the biblical ways of describing a life of discipleship pleasing to God.

As Harvard's former dean put it, "Out of the vocabulary of everyday life our religion fastened on this familiar term to give it new meanings and a new direction" (W. L. Sperry, *Those of the Way*, p. 5).

Multitudes of believers through the ages have sought to find and to pursue this way of righteousness and holiness, of virtue and sanctity. The lives of several known to history as having found and followed in this "more excellent way" of holiness are as interesting as they are challenging. Both in the Old and New Testaments God's people are ideally portrayed as "strangers and pilgrims" (1 Pet. 2:11) en route to their homeland, to a "better country" (Heb. 11:13-16). Urged by a "divine discontent," they press on toward their "high calling . . . in Christ" (Phil. 3:14). It is people like these who encourage one's faith and challenge one to a life of discipleship available to all but experienced by too few.

Several of these thumbnail sketches of the saints of yesterday have appeared in pages of the *Herald* and are here cited by permission. These were originally prepared at the request of the editor, Dr. J. C. McPheeters, and appeared over a period of 24 months. In large part they are the fruit of a doctoral dissertation, classroom courses on the subject of holy living, preaching at summer conferences, and lecturing at ministers' workshops. These are shared in the hope that they may be challenging and edifying to those who now seek to find and to share "the way of holiness."

Ancient Witnesses

1. **Clement of Rome**
(Bishop of Rome A.D. 92-101)

One of the earliest witnesses of the way of full salvation is Clement of Rome, who lived after most of, if not
all, the New Testament had been written. In a letter
addressed to the church at Corinth, which reflects the influence of the New Testament and probably his own experience, Clement wrote:

> Who is able to explain the bond of the love of God?
> . . . Love unites us to God. Love covereth a multitude of
> sins. Love beareth all things, is longsuffering in all
> things. There is nothing base, nothing haughty in love;
> love admits no schism, love makes no sedition, love
> does all things in concord. In love were all the elect of
> God made perfect. Without love is nothing well pleas-
> ing to God. . . .
>
> See, beloved, how great and wonderful is love, and
> that of its perfection there is no expression. Who is
> able to be found in it save those to whom God grants it?
> Let us then beg and pray of his mercy that we may be
> found in love, without human partisanship, free from
> blame. . . . Those who were perfected in love by the
> grace of God have a place among the pious who shall be
> made manifest at the visitation of the Kingdom of
> Christ. (I Clement 49-50, ed. K. Lake, *Apostolic
> Fathers*, vol. 1)

This epistle of Clement is perhaps closer to Paul than
any other postapostolic Christian writings. He speaks of
perfect love as the live option to those who beg and pray for
it. These, by God's grace, can be "free from blame." By
"perfect love" he means a love that is of God, shed abroad
in the heart by the Holy Spirit (Rom. 5:5), and in which
there is no element contrary to the Spirit of Christ. He

uses the term "perfect" several times, by which he means full, complete, and without blemish. While one may not be without *fault*, one can, by God's grace, be free from *blame*.

Clement wrote toward the end of the first century at a time when Christianity was experiencing its most vigorous growth. Soon it was to challenge successfully the mighty Roman Empire. Jesus' way of love and truth prevailed over a sophisticated and entrenched paganism. This can happen again!

2. **Ignatius of Antioch** (A.D. 67-107)

An early witness of the way of full salvation was the bishop of the important church of Antioch in Syria. This church, perhaps the most influential in the New Testament, was the first to incorporate Gentiles into its membership as a matter of policy, and sponsored the first foreign missionary service (Acts 11:20-26; 13:1-3). Bishop Ignatius wrote several letters which still provide interesting and edifying reading. One of these is addressed to the Ephesians, probably while Ignatius was on the road to Rome, where he expected to receive a martyr's crown. He was determined that nothing should prevent him from this event. To him and to his contemporaries martyrdom represented the highest expression of Christian fidelity and love.

Paul had assured his readers that Christians are temples of the Holy Spirit. He urged believers to be "filled with the Spirit" (Eph. 5:18). It is sometimes observed that in justification Christ is *for* us, while in sanctification Christ is *in* us. In any case, God's temple must be holy to be a fit dwelling place for the Holy Spirit. Even Solomon realized that "the most High dwelleth not in temples made with hands" (Acts 7:48; cf. 2 Chron. 2:6).

18

Perhaps influenced by the vigorous metaphors of Peter and Paul, Ignatius wrote:

> You are as stones of the temple of the Father, made ready for the building of God our Father, carried up to the heights by the engine of Jesus Christ, that is the cross, and using as a rope the Holy Spirit. And your faith is your windlass and love is the road which leads up to God. You are then all fellow travelers, and carry with you God, and the Temple, and Christ, and holiness, and are in all ways adorned by commandments of Jesus Christ. . . . Let us therefore do all things as though He were dwelling in us, that we may be His temples, and that He may be our God in us. (*To the Ephesians*, 9, 14-15)

That Christians should be shrines indwelt by God himself is the life to which every believer is summoned. In the expectation of victory over sin, Ignatius is obviously influenced by the First Epistle of John: "No one who abides in him sins" (1 John 3:9, author's translation). That the believer is to be a shrine inhabited by the Holy Spirit reflects the language of Paul: "You are temples of the Holy Spirit" (cf. 1 Cor. 6:19). That the believer should seek to be a temple indwelt by God himself is the bold expectation of Eph. 3:19.

From Paul, through Ignatius, comes to us the summons to personal sanctity made possible only by God himself. As a bishop, Ignatius, like Paul, exerted considerable influence through letters written to his churches. His witness reveals that he was a great administrator; in addition, though hounded by a hostile government, he gave priority to inner sanctity.

3. **Polycarp of Smyrna** (A.D. 69-155)

A second-century witness of "the way" is the bishop of Smyrna, Polycarp by name. In this century, more than perhaps any other, the infant Church was faced with two formidable foes. The subtle temptations from within threatened the nature of the Church and its mission. The brutal pressures from the political system without tried to intimidate and to stifle it. The Gnostics sought to turn the Church into a philosophical sect. The legalists (Ebionites) attempted to bind it to the past and make it a sect of Judaism. Christianity was outlawed, and to confess Christ became a capital offense punishable by death. Yet in spite of this the Church grew and flourished.

Polycarp lived and preached a triumphant Christian life. In a letter addressed to the church at Philippi he wrote, "If any one is inwardly possessed of these graces, he hath fulfilled the command of righteousness, since he that hath love is far from all sin."

Polycarp died a martyr to the faith he proclaimed. As he was brought before the Roman tribunal and urged to deny Christ as a price of life, he replied: "For 86 years have I been His servant, and He has done me no wrong; and how can I blaspheme my King who has saved me?" As he was led to the stake and the flames circled around him, he was heard to pray for his enemies. He asked the blessing of God upon them and praised the Lord for the privilege of thus sealing his testimony with his death.

His life and death constitute one of the great phases in the life of the Church. As historian T. R. Glover truly said, the early Christians "outthought, outlived, and outdied the pagans." As a result many unbelievers were led to inquire into the reason why these Christians could die so victoriously and even pray for their assassins. Many who thus inquired out of curiosity became convinced and were converted to Christianity.

Jesus, Stephen, and Polycarp prayed for their enemies prior to being put to death. As wonderful as it is to die for one's faith, it is even greater to intercede for one's murderers. Only a divinely implanted perfection of love enables one to do this; yet if it is possible for some to experience this, it is possible for all.

4. Epistle to Diognetus (A.D. 145)

The fourth witness is an unknown writer who gave a classic description of a Christian. The Christians were described by the historian Harnack as a "third race." They could not be identified by their language, their clothing, their nationality, the color of their skin, or their place of origin. They were not identifiable by their status in society or by their vocation. Since they were such a novelty, and the basis for their identification was so unusual, their contemporaries found it difficult to categorize them. An anonymous writer of the second century described Christians in language which has become classic. Among other things he said:

> For Christians are not distinguished from the rest of mankind by country, or by speech, or by customs. For they do not dwell in cities of their own, or use a different language, or practice a peculiar life. This knowledge of theirs has not been discovered by the thought and effort of inquisitive men; they are not champions of a human doctrine, as some men are. But while they dwell in Greek or barbarian cities according as each man's lot was cast, and follow the customs of the land in clothing and food, and other matters of daily life, yet the condition of citizenship which they exhibit is wonderful, and admittedly beyond all expectation.
>
> They live in countries of their own, but simply as sojourners; they share the life of citizens, they endure the lot of foreigners; every foreign land is to them a fatherland, and every fatherland a foreign land. They marry like the rest of the world, they beget children, but they do not cast their offspring adrift. They have a common table, but not a common bed. They exist

in the flesh, but they do live not after the flesh. They spend their existence upon earth, but their citizenship is in heaven. They obey the established laws, but in their own lives they surpass the laws. They love all men, and are persecuted by all.

They are unknown, and yet they are condemned; they are put to death, and yet they give proof of new life. They are poor, and yet make many rich; they lack everything, and yet in everything they abound. They are dishonoured, and their dishonour becomes their glory; they are reviled, and yet are vindicated. They are abused, and they bless; they are insulted, and repay insult with honour. They do good, and are punished as evil-doers; and in their punishment they rejoice as finding new life therein. The Jews war against them as aliens; the Greeks persecute them; and yet they that hate them can state no ground for their enmity.

In a word, what the soul is in the body Christians are in the world. The soul is spread through all the members of the body; so are Christians through all the cities of the world. The soul dwells in the body, and yet it is not of the body; so Christians dwell in the world and yet they are not of the world. The soul, itself invisible, is detained in a body which is visible; so Christians are recognized as being in the world, but their religious life remains invisible. The flesh hates the soul, and fights against it, though suffering no wrong, because it is prevented by the soul from indulging in its pleasures; so too the world, though suffering no wrong, hates the Christians because they set themselves against its pleasures.

The soul loves the flesh that hates it, and the members thereof; so Christians love them that hate them. The soul is enclosed within the body, and itself holds the body together; so too Christians are held fast in the world as in a prison, and yet it is they who hold the world together. Immortal itself, the soul abides in a mortal tenement; Christians dwell for a time amid corruptible things, awaiting their incorruption in heaven. The soul when it is stinted of food and drink thrives the better; so Christians when they are punished increase daily all the more. So great is the position to which God has appointed them, and which it is not lawful for them to refuse. (Epistle to Diognetus, chap. 5)

As the pagans viewed the strange life of Christians, many of them concluded that the explanation was supernatural, and they in turn embraced what they recognized was the superior quality. The way of holiness has a certain beauty characterized by a self-authenticating quality. Peter said this is a powerful witness to the non-Christians (1 Pet. 3:13).

5. **Tatian** (A.D. 175)

Another witness to the way of holiness is perhaps the first to write specifically on the subject of Christian perfection, at least as far as we know. A tract by Tatian is entitled "Perfection According to the Saviour." It is a sermon or essay based upon Jesus' statement to the rich young ruler to the effect that "if you would be perfect, go, sell what you possess and give to the poor, and you will have treasure in heaven" (see Matt. 19:21). The young man "went away sorrowful: for he had great possessions" (v. 22). In this remarkable tract the author says, among other things, that Christian perfection means separation from the world, maturity in Christ, and likeness to Jesus. In the words of Tatian, "Our Saviour . . . opened to us the gladsome treasure of his mouth . . . And if we sit down and ponder the glories and treasures of his Father, our heart is wonderstruck, beside itself in glad amaze, while anxiety and fear are mingled therewith for the prize that we have found."

The editor of this ancient tract commented, "He [Tatian] is a mystic and has the Kingdom within him" (J. R. Harris, ed., "Perfection According to the Saviour,"

The Bulletin of the John Rylands Library, 6, no. 1 [1924]: 23).

It seems clear that the author of this essay knew by experience the grace of God of which he writes so forcefully. No doubt he experienced what Paul describes in Rom. 5:5 as the "love of God . . . shed abroad" in the heart and the awareness of being filled with God himself.

This treatise was published before Christian perfection was perverted by alien influences foreign to the gospel period. One of the most serious of these influences was dualism; not the dualism of the Bible (between good and evil), but rather a metaphysical dualism—between light and darkness, between spirit and matter. According to this philosophy, matter is intrinsically evil, and the only way to have righteousness is to get rid of matter. It has many points in common with contemporary Christian Science.

This belief led to two quite different consequences: One was that since the body and the spirit are separate, what one does in the body does not affect the soul. Thus, the sins of the body are not regarded as having affected the pure soul imprisoned in the body. This, of course, leads to license. The other extreme leads to asceticism—the attempt on the part of earnest but misguided people to suppress their bodily needs in the hope of purifying their souls. In spite of these hazards, the Christian witness persisted through the centuries—too often, however, in a watered-down and sometimes perverted manner.

6. Clement of Alexandria (A.D. 200)

One of the most influential leaders of the Early Church was Clement of Alexandria. He flourished about a century after Clement of Rome. When John Wesley was a young man in quest of the holy life, he read "with much admiration" Clement's description of a perfect Christian. In 1741 Wesley published one of his first essays which is entitled "The Character of a Methodist" (*Journal*, 5:197). In this he undertook to draw his conception of an ideal Christian, patterned after Clement's, only "in a more scriptural manner," as he said. Clement was a Christian scholar to whom the pagans came to study paganism or their pre-Christian classics. In addition to knowing pagan literature, Clement knew Christianity and its power to deliver from sin. In his talks to the students at the Catechetical School at Alexandria, Egypt, he dwelt at length on the importance of going on unto perfection and described the qualities to be found in a full-grown Christian.

"Ought we then to be perfect, as the Father wills?" he inquires. Then he affirms, "Now the Father wishes us to be perfect by living blamelessly according to the obedience of the gospel." The Christian, he asserts, is "holy, God-bearing and God-borne. Now the Scripture, showing that sinning is foreign to him . . . plainly pronounces sin foreign and contrary to the nature of God" (Stromata, 13; cf. 1 Cor. 3:16). Against those who asserted that they could sin and still be Christians, Clement insisted that, negatively, salvation means deliverance from sin and, positively, knowing, seeing, and loving God as revealed in Christ. He was the first Christian leader of note, after the first century, to see that the central thing in Christianity is love to God and man.

7. Cyprian of Carthage (A.D. 250)

One of the most prominent Christian leaders of the third century was Cyprian, bishop of Carthage. Before his conversion he had been a wealthy and influential man of affairs. He testified that after his conversion the Holy

Spirit baptized him and filled him, enabling him henceforth to live victoriously over sin. He expressed it thus:

> As I myself was held in bonds by the innumerable errors of my previous life, from which I did not believe that I could possibly be delivered, so I was disposed to acquiesce in my clinging vices, but after that, by the help of the water of new birth, the stain of former years had been washed away, and a light from above, serene and pure, had been infused into my reconciled heart—after that, by the agency of the Spirit breathed from heaven, a second birth had restored me to a new man—then, in a wondrous manner, doubtful things at once began to assure themselves to me, hidden things to be revealed . . . what had been thought impossible, to be capable of being achieved; so that I was enabled to acknowledge that what previously, being born of the flesh, had been living in the practice of sins . . . had now to be of God, and was animated by the Spirit of holiness.

No writer in the Ancient Church is clearer in his repeated statements that following the infilling of the Holy Spirit the Christian need not sin, although he is yet subject to temptation and needs to watch and pray.

Although Cyprian testified to cleansing from sin at the time of his baptism with the Holy Spirit, he was careful to emphasize the necessity for humility and prayerfulness lest the "old enemy" creep upon one again. He assured his correspondents, however, that,

> depending on God with your whole strength and with your whole heart . . . liberty and power to do is given you in proportion to the increase of your spiritual grace . . . The Spirit freely flowing forth is restrained by no limits . . . Let our heart only be athirst, and be ready to receive; in the degree in which we bring to it a capacious faith, in that measure we draw from it an overflowing grace.

Cyprian speaks further of the Spirit-filled life in simple eloquence:

As the sun shines spontaneously, as the day gives light, as the fountain flows, as the shower yields moisture, so does the heavenly Spirit infuse itself into us. When the soul . . . had recognized its Author, it rises higher than the sun, and far transcends all this earthly power, and begins to be that which it believes itself to be.

He continues,

Ceilings enriched with gold, and houses adorned with mosaics of costly marble, will seem mean to you, now when you know that it is you yourself who are rather to be perfected, you who are to be adorned, and that that dwelling in which God has dwelt as in a temple, in which the Holy Spirit has begun to make his abode, is of more importance than all others. (Epistle I)

It is clearly evident that Cyprian believed a Christian should have continual victory over sin. This North African bishop exemplified the truth that "to the extent that we consecrate, the Spirit sanctifies." Another has remarked that "God giveth His Spirit unto us in the measure that we give ourselves to Him."

8. **Macarius of Egypt** (A.D. 300)

On his transatlantic voyage John Wesley read the sermons of Macarius, the Egyptian monk, "and sang." Later Wesley published extracts in the first volume of his Christian Library. R. N. Flew says that "it would have been well if later mysticism had followed Macarius rather than Augustine." The religion of Macarius was Christ-centered. To him the realization of the grace of God produced wonder. The following is his attempt to describe his experience:

The inner man regards all men with a pure eye, and the man rejoices over all the world, and desires that all should worship and love, Greeks and Jews. At another moment, like the king's son, he is as bold in the Son of God as in a father, and doors are opened unto him, and he enters into many mansions . . . other new wonders are again disclosed to him, and he is entrusted as a son and an heir, with things that cannot be told by mankind, or put into syllables by mouth and tongue. Glory to God. Amen.

Macarius believed that "the soul may be at times 'perfectly delivered from the passions of shame and be made pure through grace'" (Flew, *The Idea of Perfection*). He believed that refraining from sin was not enough, but that indwelling sin must be destroyed. The method is through Christ: "Purity of heart can be gained in no other way than through him who was crucified." Amen!

9. **Augustine, Bishop of Hippo** (A.D. 354-430)

No one understood Paul and the New Testament doctrine of grace better than Augustine. His description of his conversion is one of the devotional classics of the ages. His account of his mother, Monica—her prayers for a wayward son, her rejoicing at his conversion, and her triumphant death—is one of the choicest tributes to a Christian mother's influence. Probably the Protestant doctrine of salvation by faith has been influenced more by four men than by all other Christian writers combined— Paul, Augustine, Luther, and Wesley.

Augustine said that at his conversion he felt like a helpless chip that had been washed up from a stormy sea and that had landed securely upon a rock—the rock of divine grace. However, in his emphasis upon man's helplessness and sinfulness Augustine limited the grace of God. He did not think complete deliverance from sin possible in this life. Even at that, many of his statements are surprisingly close to the Wesleyan position.

Like Cyprian and others of that period, Augustine believed that the gift of the Holy Spirit was to be expected following baptism. Said he, "The dove in Christ's baptism did represent and prefigure our unction [anointing], that is, the Holy Spirit coming on us after baptism." He always thought of the Holy Spirit as divine love. "By the Holy Spirit, which is given . . . by imposition of hands . . . 'The love of God is shed abroad in our hearts by the Holy Ghost which is given unto us.'" Augustine believed that the Holy Spirit dwelt within him and directed him in the messages which he delivered to his congregation.

10. **John Cassian** (A.D. 370-435)

In the early centuries of the Christian era, Greek and Persian ideas produced the conviction that the body is inherently evil. The resulting belief was that no complete deliverance from sin could be expected in this life. This led to asceticism, and asceticism plus Christian ideals produced monasticism—"the greatest organized quest for perfection in history."

Among the monks, John Cassian had ideas on holiness that often approached the New Testament emphasis on evangelical perfection. Said Cassian, "Perfection is not arrived at simply by self-denial . . . unless there is that charity . . . which consists in purity of heart alone" ("Conferences," P.N.F., 6:297).

Medieval Witnesses

A.D. 500—1500

When one considers the extent to which the noblest people of the Middle Ages went in pursuit of holiness, it may well put us to shame. So ardent was the passion for righteousness that with many no discipline of body or mind was too great. A recital of their austerities would be pathetic, amusing, and often revolting. At the same time the history of early monasticism is a most impressive testimony of the inherent power of the Christian ideal of holiness. For the devout, the pursuit of perfection in love became a lifelong task. Not until Wesley's day did the church rediscover the biblical doctrine that we are sanctified as well as justified by faith. Holiness of heart is not a reward but a gift of grace, "lest any man should boast."

During the 1,000 years often called the Dark Ages, most of those who sought Christian perfection were "the religious," that is, those who were in religious orders or the clergy. The institution of monasticism was usually associated with the quest for a deeper and more vital Christian life. Mysticism was then very influential, and it was the mystics who were particularly linked with vital Christianity. Witnesses to a deeper work of grace subsequent to regeneration were very few in number. Their witness is therefore the more prized because unusual.

11. **Bernard of Clairvaux** (1090-1153)

One of the great saints of the Middle Ages was Bernard, founder of the monastery of Clairvaux. He was one of the most influential men of his day. His influence lives on in such hymns as "O Sacred Head Now Wounded," "Jesus, the Very Thought of Thee," and "Jerusalem the Golden." The center of his religious thought and sermons was Jesus the Crucified. From this influence came Gerhardt's hymns, Zinzendorf's emphasis on Christ as Savior, and the subsequent emphasis on Christ, instead of the church, as the center of Christian life.

His spiritual power is due to the training of a godly mother, resulting in his conversion at an early age and his subsequent zeal in following what he felt to be the truth. His pure life was perhaps the most effective argument against the corrupt church of his day. To Bernard "what went to a man's heart and sanctified it was true in theology." Christian experience was a better test of theology than reason; meditation was better than logic; love was the chief thing in Christianity.

In spite of the errors of the church which he defended, his emphasis on heart purity as the path to truth paved the way for Luther's ideas and for those of Pietism and Methodism.

12. **Francis of Assisi** (1182-1226)

Few Christians have followed as literally the life-style of Jesus as did Francis of Assisi. Few have exerted as wide an influence on Catholics, Protestants, and others as the founder of the Franciscan order.

Francis was a shining light of the Middle Ages. His simple life of renunciation, poverty, helpfulness, and evangelism has often been compared to the earthly life of his Lord. As the son of a wealthy merchant, he early became convinced of the vanity of life. His conversion is placed at the time when he saw a leper and decided to help him instead of "passing by on the other side."

The second crisis in his spiritual experience came when he heard a voice saying in the words of Jesus, "If thou wilt be perfect, go and sell that thou hast, and give to the poor, and thou shalt have treasure in heaven; and come and follow me" (Matt. 19:21). No man ever obeyed this command more literally and earnestly. Immediately he gave away his inheritance to the poor and went as a traveling preacher over much of Europe and even to the Mohammedans in the Holy Land. His unselfish life inspired others to do likewise, and soon numerous followers became evangelists of the simple gospel of Christ's love for all mankind. A sense of need, a dedication of one's ransomed powers, and a steadfast devotion resulted in a strong and beautiful life then, just as it does now. "He that loseth his life for my sake shall find it" (Matt. 10:39).

13. John Tauler (1300?-1361)

"I pray thee, simply for God's sake, to counsel me how I shall . . . attain to the highest perfection that a man may reach on earth." Such was the prayer of Master Tauler.

John Tauler is known as one of the most powerful preachers of medieval times. Some time after his first religious awakening, when he had become widely known as a religious leader, a Friend of God, whose name is lost to modern history, discerned Tauler's spiritual lack and frankly told the popular preacher that his religion was external and that his sermons were powerless. Tauler was meek enough and honest enough to acknowledge the truth of this faithful rebuke. He then spent two years in retirement, confessing the sin of his heart and praying for cleansing. His prayers were answered, and he experienced a mighty purifying baptism of the Holy Spirit.

Tauler was then about 50 years of age. From then on he preached with vastly increased power and effectiveness. As Schaff observes, he stressed henceforth the work of the Holy Spirit in "enlightening and sanctifying" the inner life. Extensive revivals followed. He ranks among the first of that illustrious group of men of the 14th century known as the Brethren of the Common Life, who so greatly influenced Luther and Wesley.

Said Tauler in a sermon for Thursday of Holy Week, "Christ is the Master of perfection, wherefore a man shall leave all things to follow Him, for in God we find all things united in one perfectness . . . Therefore, O man, if thou wilt be perfect, be a follower of Christ. . . . Therefore forsake the creatures, and follow after the Maker of Perfection" (*History and Life of Dr. John Tauler* [New York: 1858], p. 341).

14. **Thomas a Kempis** (1380-1471)

Thomas a Kempis, from whom Wesley learned that religion is of the heart, was a member of the Brethren of the Common Life of the 14th century. The quest for perfection in the medieval church found expression in three great movements: asceticism, which resulted in monasticism; the preaching orders, such as the Franciscan; and later, the Friends of God and the Brethren—the nearest approach to evangelical perfection before the Reformation.

Thomas recognized clearly the need for cleansing of the sinful nature as well as the forgiveness of sins. Said he,

> Since then our inward affection is much corrupted, our actions thence proceeding must needs be corrupted also . . . O Lord my God, who has created me after

thine own image and likeness, grant me this grace, which thou hast showed to be so great and so necessary to salvation; that I may overcome my most evil nature which draweth me to sin and to perdition.

Like Wesley years later, he saw clearly the need for cleansing from the carnal mind, but he failed to discover that cleansing may come instantaneously—by faith in Christ!

The Widener Library at Harvard University (largest university library in the world) has an astonishing number of volumes and translations in various languages and editions of the classic which Thomas wrote and edited, *The Imitation of Christ*.

Witnesses of the Sixteenth and Seventeenth Centuries

These two centuries were ones of change, ferment, innovation, renaissance, reformation, and revolution. Nothing was quite the same in western Europe thereafter. Among the changes in the 16th century were the intellectual Renaissance, the Protestant Reformation, the Peasants' Revolt in Germany, the adoption of the inductive method in science, and the exploration of North and South America. The movements of the 16th century were mostly of the mind and heart—the Renaissance and the Reformation.

The movements of the 17th century were more political though religion was often the underlying motive. For instance, the Thirty Years' War in Europe was between Catholics and Protestants. And in England, the conflict was between the Established Church and the Puritans. Purely political, however, was the struggle between European powers for dominance in the New World.

During these centuries the basic issues were survival and the stress on the nature of the Christian life. In the centuries later theological emphasis shifted from a stress on justification to a stress on sanctification, from the nature of faith to the fruits of faith.

15. Johann von Staupitz (1440-1524)

Medieval mystics such as Bernard and Francis stressed love as central in Christianity. Luther and the other Reformers stressed faith. In a midway position stood Tauler and Johann von Staupitz. The latter "directed Luther from his sins to the merits of Christ, from the study of the law to the cross, from works to faith, from scholasticism to the study of the Scriptures."

Said Staupitz, "Divine love is not from man, nor law, nor the letter of Scriptures which kills, but from the Holy Spirit who reveals God's love in Christ to our heart and fills it" (Schaff).

From him Luther learned of salvation by simple faith in Christ. Later, when Staupitz saw the fanaticism among some of the Reformers, he turned back toward the Catholic church and stressed the necessity of good works along with faith. He was afraid that those who stressed faith alone would abolish the law. We can appreciate, however, his insistence that "the love of God and the imitation of Christ" are the ruling ideas in Christian piety. Wesley joined this emphasis on the love of God and the imitation of Christ with Luther's emphasis on faith as the means. Thus, while developing his doctrine of Christian perfection, Wesley avoided the danger of lawlessness and self-righteousness by insisting that entire sanctification, as well as justification, is by faith.

16. Martin Luther (1483-1546)

From Paul to Augustine to Luther to Wesley is a line of spiritual descent that stresses a religion of the heart.

"But," Wesley asked, "who understood justification as clearly as Luther, yet who misunderstood sanctification

39

as much as he?" In Luther justification and sanctification were "fused and confused," as historians have pointed out.

Martin Luther placed the major stress on justification by faith rather than upon sanctification. This is partly explained by his aversion to mysticism, by his reaction from the extremists of his day, and by an exclusive attention to the basis of justification rather than its effects. Hence a great many have rightly felt that the Reformation did not go far enough in the direction of New Testament piety.

Nevertheless Luther, especially in his early writings, expressed some deeply spiritual insights. He said much about the importance of proving faith by works.

> Thus from faith flow forth love, and joy in the Lord, and from love a cheerful, willing, free spirit, disposed to serve our neighbor voluntarily, without taking any account of gratitude or ingratitude, praise or blame, gain or loss . . . love is quickly diffused in our hearts through the Spirit, and by love we are made free, joyful, all-powerful, active workers, victors over all our tribulations, servants to our neighbor, and nevertheless lords of all things . . . Each should become to the other a sort of Christ, so that we may be mutually Christ's, and that the same Christ may be in all of us: that is, that we may be truly Christian.

He thus defined the true Church: "They are called a Christian people, and have the Holy Ghost, who daily sanctifies them, not only by the forgiveness of sin, but also by the laying aside, expelling and destroying of sin, and hence they are also called a holy people."

17. Caspar Schwenkfeld (1489-1561)

Caspar Schwenkfeld was a Silesian nobleman of the 16th century who felt that Luther had not given enough emphasis to the sanctification of the believer. He felt that it was not sufficient to experience justification by faith and that the believer is under as great an obligation to pursue holiness as the sinner to seek salvation. He criticized the Lutherans for lack of discipline, insisting that separation from the world and purity of life are indispensable in a true Christian.

He followed Staupitz and the medieval mystics in emphasizing the love of God as central in the Christian life. Like Wesley he emphasized three kinds of Christians: "children," or beginners in the love of God; "young men," or those more advanced; and "fathers," or those made perfect in love (cf. 1 John 2:12-14). He did not place emphasis on faith as the means of entire sanctification but stressed the gradual process and mentioned suffering as a means of purification. He warned against assuming that one can "please God by merely having faith in Christ, yet never advancing in devotion or sanctification" (J. Wach, *Journal of Religion*, January, 1946).

He objected to the idea of imputed righteousness only of the believer and insisted on the need of an actual or imparted righteousness. Thus Schwenkfeld anticipated the Pietists and Methodists in his emphasis on purity of life, on discipline as well as on a creed, upon "Christ in us" as well as "Christ for us." To him the experience of the living Christ was central, and it must result in a life like that of Christ.

Schwenkfeld's influence on the Reformation has not received the attention it deserves. This lack has been met in part by the attention given him by Prof. Joachim Wach of the University of Chicago. Historically Schwenkfeld's emphasis on holy living is the link between Lutheranism and Pietism.

18. Brother Lawrence (Nicholas Herman)
(1611-91)

Christians in the New Testament are often called "holy ones" *(hagioi)*. None better deserve this title than a French chef of the 17th century.

A cook, especially a cook for an institution, has many temptations to impatience. This French chef, who lived during the troubled Thirty Years' War, acquired an international reputation for practicing the presence of God for 40 years in the midst of his culinary duties. His name was Nicholas Herman of Lorraine, better known as Brother Lawrence.

Like John Inskip he found the secret of holiness to lie in a determination to be "wholly and forever" the Lord's; like Wesley he early discovered that true religion consists in purity of intention. In a letter explaining how he arrived at a "habitual sense of God's presence," he explained:

> Having found in many books different methods of going to God, and divers practices of the spiritual life, I thought this would serve rather to puzzle me than facilitate what I sought after, which was nothing else than how to become wholly God's. This made me resolve to give the all for the all; so after having given myself wholly to God, . . . I renounced, for the love of him, everything that was not his, and I began to live as if there was none but he and I in the world.
>
> Sometimes I considered myself before him as a poor criminal at the feet of his judge; at other times I beheld him in my heart as my Father, as my God. I worshipped him the oftenest that I could, keeping my mind in his holy presence, and recalling it as often as I found it wandering from him . . . this not only hinders our offending him . . . but it also begets in us a holy freedom, . . . and a familiarity with God, wherewith we ask, and that successfully, the graces we stand in need of.

42

The language of wholehearted Christian devotion is a universal language.

19. George Fox, the First Quaker (1624-91)

Fox was a pioneer in what has been described as "social mysticism." Fox was a mystic, but more. He did not seek solitude and personal perfection only, but also projected this concern into the conscience of his countrymen. His example and enthusiasm were contagious.

While Spener was meeting the more spiritual members of his German Lutheran congregation in midweek class meetings, George Fox was disturbing complacent English congregations with his exhortations to personal sanctity. As a shoemaker young Fox longed for peace of mind and communion with God. Counsel with clergymen as to his spiritual condition brought no relief; one prescribed tobacco, another physic and blood-letting—all were "miserable comforters." At length he heard an inner voice which whispered, "There is one, even Christ Jesus, that can speak to thy condition; and when I heard it my heart did leap for joy" *(Journal)*. From this time on Fox began to preach with assurance and power, but still was harassed by doubts and longed for a deeper work of grace. About the year 1648 he wrote:

> Now was I come up in Spirit through the flaming sword, into the paradise of God . . . I knew nothing but pureness, and innocency, and righteousness, being renewed into the image of God by Christ Jesus, to the state of Adam, which he was in before he fell.

Later he recorded:

> I found none that could bear to be told that any should come to Adam's perfection, into that image of God, that righteousness and holiness that Adam was in before he fell; to be clear and pure without sin as he was.

Apparently the witness to and exposition of holiness was not a popular theme. Because Fox was not concerned with theology, the movement which he inspired has tolerated a wide range of theological positions. Subjectivity needs balancing with sound doctrine. But none in this spiritual succession have stressed *both* inward and outward holiness more than the Society of Friends.

20. **Philipp Jakob Spener** (1635-1705)

The 17th century in Europe was characterized by religious controversy and Protestant scholasticism. The latter term describes the tendency to define and defend theology rather than promote godly living. One Lutheran pastor reacted against this dead orthodoxy by preaching "awakening sermons" to his congregation. This pastor, called the father of Pietism, and hence a spiritual ancestor of English Methodism, was Philipp Jakob Spener.

After reading the Bible and Arndt's book on *True Christianity,* he saw that New Testament piety is more than a dead orthodoxy. Over against the prevailing Lutheranism "he emphasized sanctification rather than justification, communion with God rather than reconciliation with him, Christ *in* us as well as Christ *for* us" (Nagler, *Pietism and Methodism*). As a result of presenting the Bible as a pattern for living, as well as a pattern for belief, and stressing personal piety in midweek classes, a revival occurred in his parish the effects of which were to be felt throughout Germany, England, and the American colonies.

While he stressed sanctification along with justification, the two were "fused and confused" as with Luther, and he did not clearly teach the possibility of entire sanctification attainable instantaneously by faith. This prepares one to appreciate the significance of Wesley's contribution.

This movement known as Pietism was a reformation within Protestantism in the direction of holiness of heart and life—the recovery of the New Testament emphasis on that "holiness, without which no man shall see the Lord" (Heb. 12:14). After a span of 16 centuries it was again widely accepted that Christianity begins with a new heart and ends in a transformation of life.

From these German Pietists the Methodists acquired the "love feast," the class meeting, and the doctrine of assurance.

21. Samuel Willard (1640-1707)

Samuel Willard was a Puritan preacher, "teacher of a church [Old South Church] in Boston," about the year 1700. He preached sermons on holiness, some of which are published. He spoke of the "root of defilement in man" and asserted that "every actual sin leaves a spot, a stain, a filthiness behind it." Said he,

> There is therefore a two-fold taking away of sin, answerable to the two-fold mischief·which it doth the man, by its adhesion to him: the former is by *justification*, the latter by *sanctification*. Sin is taken away by justification, when the atonement being accepted by the sinner, he is pardoned and his guilt removed. Sin is taken away by sanctification, when God, by his Spirit applies his grace to the soul by which he mortifieth sin, and cleanseth it of the defilement which cleaveth to it.

"While the merit of Christ," he continued, "removes the guilt of sin in justification, the grace of Christ communicates sanctification." It is applied only to those "who come to him by saving faith in him." In closing, he exhorted, "Let the sense of remaining corruption, put you

45

upon the exercise of . . . sanctification, . . . and never cease from this work, till sin be no more in you, and grace be arrived at its full degree of perfection."

In his message the preacher emphasized that according to Matt. 5:48 God is perfect and, since children should be like their parents, God's children should be perfect, like their Heavenly Father. He was careful to distinguish between justification and sanctification; the former concerns man's person, the latter concerns his nature. He declared that justification deals with guilt, while sanctification deals with pollution. "Sanctification alone makes one truly blessed and happy." Thus he describes what he calls "evangelical perfection": "The sincerity, which God's children do express in their obedience, is so often called perfection in the Scripture (Job 1:1, etc.), by Reason that being offered to God with Christ's incense it finds favor with him."

Likewise: "Created holiness in man, is nothing else but that rectitude in his whole nature, and all the powers of it, whereby he is enabled and inclined to live and be to the Glory of God in all things."

As Willard saw it, "God, who loves holiness, cannot be well pleased with anything that he seeth in us, that is of another tincture. To 'grow in grace' (2 Pet. 3:18) implies that there is a new principle of holiness infused into us; for we must have grace in us, before we can grow into it."

(This is from Samuel Willard, "Evangelical Perfection," or how far the gospel requires believers to aspire after being completely perfect, as it was delivered in a lecture at Boston on June 10, 1694; *The Fountain* [Boston: 1700].)

When one considers that this comes from a Calvinist preacher, before the time of Wesley, he can agree that here indeed is a definition of "the more excellent way."

22. **Edward Pelling** (1640?-1718)

Holiness, wholeness, or perfection is the normal desire of every "awakened" person. Too often this desire becomes perverted or stifled until it vanishes. Toward the close of the 17th century there seems to have been a widespread desire for spiritual wholeness and a disgust with the superficial and corrupt in religion. This was notably true in English-speaking countries. The rise of "religious societies" in the Anglican church testified to an increasing concern with a "religion of the heart" that desired something more personal and dynamic that was normally found in church liturgy. Pelling exemplified this concern.

Edward Pelling was rector of Petworth in Sussex and chaplain-in-ordinary to His Majesty. In 1695 a sermon on holiness was published. In it he urged the importance of making holiness "the business of our lives." Said he,

> Particular, true, substantial, internal, personal holiness is indispensably requisite to us men, in order to our everlasting peace.
>
> There must be a personal holiness of our own, as a necessary condition to prepare us for the righteousness which is imputative; that is, we must make piety and virtue the business of our lives, to dispose and fit us for God's gracious acceptance at our lives' end. This is the middle way between the papist on the one hand who build on Works without Imputation; and those on the other hand, who rely upon Imputation without any Works, unless it be the single work of Faith.

John Wesley, a generation later, was also to insist on the "middle road" between the "means of grace" and "faith alone," and to preach *sanctification by faith.*

23. **Madame Guyon** (1648-1717)

This French mystic led a life of such devotion that her witness has transcended creed, nationality, time, and language.

Madame Guyon, a Roman Catholic, was called "a Quaker born out of due time"; so emphatically did she testify to the quiet influence of the Holy Spirit in purifying the heart and life. At the age of 20 (in 1668) she received a definite assurance of salvation by faith in Christ. After this experience she rejoiced in nothing so much as fervent and continual prayer. Later came periods of darkness and temptation to worldliness, during which time she met a "poor man" who told her that

> God required not merely a heart of which it could only be said it is forgiven, but a heart which could . . . be designated as *holy*, that it was not sufficient to escape hell, but that he demanded also the subjection of the evil of our nature, and the utmost purity and height of Christian attainment.

After several years of seeking for this inward cleansing she experienced entire sanctification and the filling of the Holy Spirit by faith so that instead of peace she now had "the God of peace." She testified, "One characteristic of this higher degree of experience was a sense of inward purity." Revivals of "pure and undefiled religion" then occurred all over France because of her godly influence. Her life indicates that God has His witness to full victory over sin and perfection in love in nearly every generation.

Eighteenth-Century
Witnesses

24. William Tennent (1673-1746)

The first and perhaps the most powerful revival of religion that has swept over America was the Great Awakening in 1734-44. It had four distinct phases: in Nova Scotia, in New England, in the middle Atlantic colonies, and in the southern colonies. In this whole movement the individual who probably exerted the greatest lasting influence on the revival was not Jonathan Edwards but William Tennent. It is said that the secret of Tennent's power was the fact that after he believed he was "sealed with the Holy Spirit of promise." It was he who trained both his own sons and many students in his "log college," and they promoted powerful revivals wherever they preached. History affords no more convincing argument for Christian schools as agencies for evangelism than Tennent's "log college." These colleges were the antecedents of Princeton University.

> On one occasion, during the interval of worship on the Sabbath, Mr. William Tennent retired to a grove nearby, for private meditation and prayer. When the congregation reassembled, and their pastor did not appear, several individuals went to the grove to find him. They found him lying helpless on the ground, under the power of the visions of God which had there opened upon his mind. In their arms they carried him to the pulpit, so that he might tell the people of the "glory manifested to him." The prayer was answered, and "no man" not thus illuminated "ever spake as did this man" on that occasion. Such manifestations were of common occurrence in the experience of these men, and they ever spoke and acted under their influence. (Asa Mahan, *Baptism of the Holy Ghost,* p. 84)

"Is not Thy grace as mighty now . . .?"

25. **Christian David** (1690-1751)

Christian David was born in Moravia of Catholic parents and became an evangelical Christian as the result of searching the Scriptures and of listening to the prayers of a Lutheran pastor during a long illness. Later he led scores of persecuted Moravians to the shelter of Count von Zinzendorf's Herrnhut (the Lord's House) in Silesia.

After seeking holiness of heart diligently since 1725, John Wesley found himself in the summer of 1738 in Germany visiting the home of the Brethren or Moravians. Here he found kindred spirits who claimed to have found the experience of a "clean new heart" for which he himself had so long sought. He listened eagerly to their experiences, then wrote down what he remembered of their joyous words of testimony to full salvation. Here is the testimony of Christian David, first leader of the Herrnhut Moravians, as reported by Wesley:

> I was assured my sins were forgiven . . . I saw not then that the first promise to the children of God is, "sin shall no more reign over you"; but thought I was to feel it in me no more from the time it was forgiven. Therefore, although I had the mastery over it, yet I often feared it was not forgiven, because it still stirred in me . . . because, though it did not reign, it did remain in me and I was continually tempted, though not overcome . . . Neither saw I then that the being justified freely is widely different from having the full assurance of faith. I remembered not that our Lord told his apostles before his death "ye are clean"; whereas it was not till many days after it that they were fully assured, by the Holy Ghost then received, of their reconciliation to God through his blood. (J. Wesley, *Journal*, 2:30)

In this testimony there is a clear distinction made between forgiveness and full deliverance from sin. But here, as in German Pietism generally, the doctrine of entire sanctification was confused with the witness of the Spirit to one's regeneration and adoption. Wesley, too, in his early ministry, did not make a clear distinction here as he was to do later. This indicates Wesley's keen interest in religious autobiography—the story of one's quest for a conscious experience of the "second blessing properly so-called."

26. Count Nicholas von Zinzendorf
(1700-1760)

Nicholas von Zinzendorf, nobleman, poet, and devout Christian, was a major influence among the United Brethren and the Methodists.

Zinzendorf applied himself diligently to his studies but spent his free time reading the writings of Martin Luther and talking to the professors of theology.

Upon graduation he was sent, in accordance with the custom among wealthy families of that day, on a tour. On this tour he was introduced to William of Orange and other princes and noblemen. He spent half a year in Paris. He formed a friendship with Cardinal Noailles and had long talks with him about the differences between the Catholics and the Protestants. But something which happened to him in the art gallery at Dusseldorf made the greatest impression of all.

While wandering among the pictures in the gallery, the young count came suddenly upon a picture of Christ with the crown of thorns. Beneath the picture was the Latin question: *"Hoc tibi feci; quid mihi fecisti?"* Quickly Zinzendorf translated it: "I have done this for you; what have you done for me?" The tears came to his eyes. "I have loved Him for a long time," he said to himself, "but I have never actually done anything for Him. From now on I will do whatever He leads me to do!"

Zinzendorf believed in brotherly love. He strove mightily to unite in spiritual fellowship various evangelical groups in Europe, and the Moravian missionary movement was one of the results. He was Christ-centered in his faith and zeal but was too ecumenical for some to accept his leadership.

27. **John Wesley** (1703-91)

The two most distinctive doctrines in early Methodism were the witness of the Spirit and Christian perfection.

John Wesley was a pioneer in religious autobiography. He was a keen student of human nature and carefully recorded personal testimonies. Before his day devout Christians spoke very seldom and with great caution about personal Christian experience. Even among the Pietists of Germany, personal testimony was limited to selected leaders in the congregation. Wesley, however, eagerly listened to testimonies and persuaded many to write them out for publication. Thus he sought for two things: to learn God's method of dealing with souls and to give help to those seeking full salvation. The testimonies which he collected with special interest were those concerned with a second work of grace. They helped him formulate his doctrine of Christian perfection—a doctrine based upon Scripture but interpreted in the light of Christian experience. He wrote to Dodd on February 5, 1756, as follows:

> When I began to make the Scriptures my chief study . . . I began to see that Christians are called to love God with all their heart, and to serve him with all strength; which is precisely what I apprehended to be meant by the scriptural term, "perfection" . . . You easily observe I build on no authority, ancient or modern, but the Scripture. If this supports any doctrine, it will stand: if not, the sooner it falls the better. If therefore you will please to point out to me any

passages in the sermon which are contrary to Scripture, I shall be as willing to oppose as ever I was to defend them.

His early studies in the Scriptures, his own quest for holiness, his personal Pentecost, and his observations of the lives and testimonies of others all furnished the basis for his formulation of "the most distinctive doctrine of Methodism"—entire sanctification receivable instantly by faith in Christ.

John and Charles Wesley are credited with being the chief human instruments in a reformation of the Reformation—moving from sound doctrine to transformed lives. The Evangelical Revival which so profoundly influenced the English-speaking world began with them.

The question as to whether John Wesley himself professed the experience of entire sanctification is often debated. In general it may be said that his witness to this second work of grace is almost as specific as his description of his conversion experience at Aldersgate Street. Some think Wesley received this experience at the watch night service of 1738 when a Pentecostal outpouring accompanied a meeting which lasted until 3 a.m. This appears unlikely. Another entry in his *Journal* for December 23, 1744, appears more probable as the time when he received his personal Pentecost. He said:

> In the evening, while I was reading prayers at Snowsfield, I found such light and strength as I never remember to have had before. I saw every thought as well as action or word, just as it was rising in my heart, and whether it was right before God, or tainted with pride or selfishness.
>
> I waked the next morning, by the grace of God, in the same spirit; and about eight, being with two or three that believed in Jesus, I felt such an awe, and tender sense of the presence of God, as greatly confirmed me therein; so that God was before me all the day long. I sought and found him in every place; and

could truly say, when I lay down at night, "Now I have lived a day."

In his *Journal* for October 28, 1762, he recalled:

> Many years ago my brother frequently said, "Your day of Pentecost is not fully come; but I doubt not it will; and you will then hear of persons sanctified, as frequently as you do now of persons justified." Any unprejudiced reader may observe, that it was now fully come.

In this cautious fashion he implied his personal possession of what he constantly urged upon others.

28. **Jonathan Edwards** (1703-58)

Edwards, as a theologian, has been characterized as having one of the greatest intellects of all time. He was also a saint.

It cannot be emphasized too strongly that the baptism with the Holy Spirit is the normal privilege of every Christian. It should be as definite as water baptism. John baptized with water unto repentance, but the work of Jesus is to baptize "with the Holy Spirit and with fire." How can one be completely Christian and ignore this baptism? President Jonathan Edwards thus described his baptism:

> One day, when walking for divine contemplation and prayer, I had a view, that for me was extraordinary, of the glory of the Son of God, as Mediator between God and man, and his wonderful, great, full, pure, and sweet grace and love, and meek and gentle condescension. This grace, that appeared so calm and sweet, appeared also great above the heavens; the person of Christ appeared also ineffably excellent, with an excellency great enough to swallow up all thought and conception, which continued, as near as I can judge, about an hour, which kept me the greater part of the time in a flood of tears, weeping aloud. I had an ardency of soul to be, what I know not otherwise how to

express, emptied and annihilated, to lie in the dust and
to be filled with Christ alone, to love him with a holy
and pure love, to trust in him, to live upon him, and to
be perfectly sanctified, and made pure with a divine
and heavenly purity. (Asa Mahan, *The Baptism of the
Holy Ghost,* p. 85)

A criticism often made of the modern holiness movement is that it emphasizes one's experience and subjective
condition more than Christ. It serves as a reminder that in
a wholesome presentation of the doctrine, Christ is central.
We are "complete in him" and only in Him (ibid.).

Later when Edwards wrote his treatise on "Religious
Affections," he could find no better representative of the
"more excellent way" than his own wife.

29. **Mrs. Sarah Edwards** (18th Century)

The name of Jonathan Edwards will always be linked
not only with theology but also with the Great Awakening
in New England.

It is probable that Jonathan Edwards, one of America's most distinguished theologians, married his wife,
Sarah, because of her reputation for piety. During her
married life she continued to have visions of divine glory
and would lie prostrate under the power of such visitations
of love. Before their marriage he wrote this of her:

They say there is a young lady . . . who is beloved
of that great Being who moves and rules the world,
and that there are certain seasons in which this great
Being, in some way or other invisible, comes to her,
and fills her mind with exceeding sweet delights, and
that she hardly ever cares for anything, except to medi-
tate on him; that she expects, after a while, to be received up where he is, to be raised up out of this world
and caught up into heaven, being assured that he loves
her too well to let her remain at a distance from him
always. There she is to dwell with him, and to be

ravished with his love and delight forever. Therefore, if you present all the world before her, with the richest of its treasures, she disregards it, and cares not for it, and is unmindful of any pain or affliction.

She has a strange sweetness in her mind, and singular purity in her affections; is most just and conscientious in all her conduct, and you could not persuade her to do anything wrong or sinful if you would give her all the world, lest she should offend this great Being. She is of a wonderful sweetness, calmness, and benevolence of mind. She will sometimes go about from place to place, singing devoutly, and seems to be always full of joy and pleasure, and no one knows for what.

30. **Six Christian Students at Oxford**

Pilgrims on the "more excellent way" are seldom without some persecution. Perhaps it should be thus. Godliness is always a silent rebuke to ungodliness. A quaint and instructive illustration of this was the persecution which six young Christians at Oxford University experienced in the days of Wesley and Whitefield.

While other students were often found guilty of the worst acts of immorality, drunkenness, rioting, gambling, etc., without being compelled to leave school, six Methodist students were expelled in March, 1768. They were given a trial and were convicted on the following charges:

1. James Matthews—incompetent in learned languages and a Methodist.
2. Thomas Jones—deficient in learned languages and guilty of leading in *extempore* prayer.
3. Joseph Shipman—attended illicit conventicles (Methodist meetings).
4. Benjamin Kay—attended a conventicle in a private house and claims a Christian should have the Spirit of God.

5. Erasmus Middleton—claims one should wait for the Spirit and that one is saved by faith alone.
6. (The sixth man was convicted of preaching in a barn.)

On these official charges the six students were summarily expelled! A storm of indignation resulted. Tracts and pamphlets were written in condemnation of the Oxford authorities.

31. Methodism's Mission

Early Methodists were often unduly given to self-scrutiny. Like other young movements, early Methodist conferences often examined their own mission and justification for existence.

The early Methodists were very conscious that their mission was to spread scriptural holiness. One of the paramount questions before the first annual conference of English Methodists was an inquiry as to the providential reason for raising up the people called Methodists. The answer given was that it was to reform the church and "to spread Scriptural Holiness over these lands." Years later, when Wesley had time to see his lifework in a larger perspective, he still regarded this doctrine and experience as the unique contribution of Methodism. Said he,

> Who has wrote more ably than Martin Luther on justification by faith alone? And who was more ignorant of the doctrine of sanctification, or more confused in his conceptions of it? . . . On the other hand, how many writers of the Romish church . . . have wrote strongly and scripturally on sanctification? . . . The Methodists maintain . . . the doctrines of free, full, present justification, . . . and of entire sanctification, both of heart and life, on the other: being as tenacious of inward holiness as any mystic; and of outward, as any Pharisee. (*Sermons*, 2:389)

59

Methodism's contribution to Protestant thought was thus to carry the Reformation farther, until the New Testament ideal was fully grasped and realized in experience as well as in doctrine. How strange that some modern leaders in this tradition are embarrassed that their legacy is this "more excellent way."

32. John Furz (1717-1800?)

This testimony illustrates the value of stressing personal holiness as a present possibility rather than as a slow process of growth only. The language reflects authentic witness of grace "more abundant."

Mr. John Furz, a Methodist lay preacher of the 18th century, lay sick and, as he supposed, at the point of death.

> I heard one of them say, "Now he is going." Meanwhile the cry of my heart was, "Lord, sanctify me now or never." In that instant I felt the mighty power of his sanctifying Spirit. It came down into my soul as a refining fire, purifying and cleansing from all unrighteousness. And from that instant I began to recover.
>
> But oh, how slow of heart have I been to believe, and how hard to understand the deep things of God! Before my conversion I thought, if I repented all my days, and was pardoned at last, it would be a great blessing. But when it pleased God to pardon me, I knew, "now is the accepted time; now is the day of salvation."
>
> But I had the same conceptions of sanctification that I had before of justification. I preached it as a slow gradual work. And while I did so, I gained no ground: I was easily provoked, which made me fear lest after I had preached to others I myself should be a castaway. But now, glory be to God, I feel no anger, no pride, no self-will: old things are passed away. All things are become new. Now I know, he that dwelleth

in love, dwelleth in God, and God in him! (*Lives of Early Methodist Preachers*, 5:133)

Of these early Methodist autobiographies R. N. Flew has observed that they are immortal classics in the realm of devotional literature. They are characterized by a freshness and spontaneity which marks them as descriptions of something intensely real and vital. These early Methodists sought holiness with an earnestness and persistence rarely seen even in the modern holiness movement. Finally, we note that they were as honest, earnest, and diligent in keeping this experience as in seeking it.

33. **Sampson Staniforth** (1720-99)

One of the practices which John Wesley initiated or at least accelerated was that of spiritual autobiography. It was his custom, while editor of the magazine he founded, the *Arminian*, to publish therein the life story of those whose hearts God had touched. Scholars have noticed that the publication of these chapters from the inner lives of "the saints" coincides with the romanticist movement and with the interest in the inner life which is manifest in the literature, the philosophy, and the music of the time.

One such miracle of grace was Sampson Staniforth, converted while a wild, dissolute soldier in the English army in Flanders. He was unconcerned about his soul until he attended Methodist preaching at the invitation of a Christian soldier. Thereafter he was under deep conviction for several weeks. During this time his life was radically altered—he quit swearing, drinking, gambling, stealing, and lying long before he had the assurance of sins forgiven. He attended "preaching" at every opportunity, read the Bible, prayed, and mourned his lost condition. He was a changed man as a result of being under conviction. One night on sentry duty he prayed through to the joyful assurance of salvation. Thereafter, for some 60 years his was a life of joyous victory through the most trying of circumstances. Every spare moment was spent in soul winning. He did not testify to a "second work of grace" but says once that he was troubled with a sense of his own "inward corruptions." At the age of 63 he summed it all up:

> Religion . . . is the gift of God through Christ, and the work of God by his Spirit. It is revealed in the Scripture, and is received and retained by faith, in the use of all gospel ordinances. It consists in an entire deadness to the work, and to our own will; and an entire devotedness of our souls, bodies, time, and substance to God through Jesus Christ. It is loving the Lord our God with all our hearts, and all mankind for God's sake. (*Lives*, 5:147)

34. William Hunter (1728-97)

In seeking for all the fullness of God, earnest souls often discover that they that seek Him shall find Him when they seek with all their hearts (see Jer. 29:13). Typical of such successful seekers is William Hunter, who wrote to John Wesley of his experience in 1779.

This witness is helpful in distinguishing between one who is "born again" and one who is "sanctified wholly." Definite seeking is often the condition for definite finding. Thus he reports,

> I went on for a long time, sometimes up and sometimes down, till it pleased God to bring me to hear you [Wesley] at Newcastle. While you were preaching [from 1 John 1:9] . . . I was clearly convinced of the doctrine of sanctification, and the attainableness of it. I came home with full purpose of heart, not to rest till I was made a living witness of it. I had now a clear view, (1) Of the holiness of God; and saw that sin could not dwell with him. (2) I had a clear view of the purity and

perfection of his law, which is a transcript of the Divine nature. And, (3) I felt my great unlikeness to both: and, although I felt no condemnation, yet, in view of these things, I felt much pain in my spirit, and my soul was humbled in the dust before him!

O, how I longed to be made like him; to love him with all my heart, soul, mind, and strength. I had glorious discoveries of the salvation of the soul; and I went on in joyful expectation, crying to the Lord to put me in possession of all he had purchased for me, and promised to me. Sometimes I seemed to be upon the threshold, just stepping into glorious liberty; but again fear and unbelief prevailed, and I started back. This cast my mind into great perplexity, and I often reasoned concerning the truth of the thing. (*Lives,* 2:247)

My heart consented to the whole truth, and I had clearer views of the way of attaining it, namely, by faith, than ever before. This added new vigour to my spirit, and I seemed to be more on the wing than ever. I prayed and wept at his footstool, that he would show me all his salvation. And he gave me to experience such a measure of his grace as I never knew before; a great measure of heavenly light and Divine power spread through all my soul; I found unbelief taken away out of my heart; my soul was filled with such faith as I never felt before; my love to Christ was like fire, and I had such views of him, as my life, my portion, my all, as swallowed me up; and oh, how I longed to be with him!

A change passed upon all the powers of my soul, and I felt a great increase of holy and heavenly tempers. I may say, with humility, it was as though I was emptied of all evil, and filled with heaven and God.

Thus under the influence of his power and grace, I rode upon the sky. My soul fed on angels' food, and I truly ate the bread of heaven. I had more glorious discoveries than ever of the Gospel of God our Saviour, and especially in his saving the soul from all sin. I enjoyed such an evidence of this in my mind, as put me beyond all doubt; and yet I never had such a sense of my own littleness, helplessness and unworthiness as now. So true it is, that only grace can humble the soul.

> From the time the Lord gave me to experience
> this grace, I became an advocate for the glorious doc-
> trine of Christian perfection: . . . I bear testimony of it
> wherever I go; and I never find my soul so happy as
> when I preach most upon the blessed subject.

Unlike some, he did not abandon the quest and decide
there was nothing to it. Because he *sought* he *found!*

35. **Mr. Mather** (1733-1801)

It was customary for John Wesley to ask certain
persons to write out a testimony of their personal experience. These he would publish in the *Arminian Magazine*
for the edification of Methodists and other readers. One of
Wesley's preachers complied with his request but omitted
what Wesley described as "one considerable branch of
his experience, touching what is properly termed 'the great
salvation.'" Mr. Mather replied fully and explicitly on this
point.

> What I experienced in my own soul was an in-
> stantaneous deliverance from all those wrong tempers
> and affections which I had long and sensibly groaned
> under; an entire disengagement from every creature,
> with an entire devotedness to God: and from that
> moment, I found an unspeakable pleasure in doing the
> will of God in all things. I had also a power to do it,
> and the constant approbation both of my own con-
> science and of God. I had a simplicity of heart, and a
> single eye to God, at all times and in all places; with
> such a fervent zeal for the glory of God and the good of
> souls, as swallowed up every other care and
> consideration . . .
> As to the manner wherein this work was wrought,
> after I was clearly justified, I was soon made sensible
> of my want of it. For although I was enabled to be very
> circumspect, and had a continual power over inward
> and outward sin, yet I felt in me what I knew was
> contrary to the mind which was in Christ, and what

hindered me from enjoying and glorifying him as I saw it was the privilege of a child of God to do . . . I was unwilling to offer up every Isaac, and inflamed with great ardour in wrestling with God; determined not to let him go; till he emptied me of all sin, and filled me with himself. This I believe he did, when I ventured upon Jesus as sufficient to save from the uttermost. He wrought in me what I cannot express, what I judge it is impossible to utter.

I was not long without reasoning; not concerning the work [of entire sanctification]—of this I was absolutely sure; but whether such and such things as I soon discovered in myself were consistent with it. And this had its use, as it qualified me to advise others, who, though saved from sin, were tried in the same way.

Upon this head I consulted Mr. Walsh, and his advice helped me in some degree; but God helped me much more in private prayer. Herein I was clearly satisfied, (1) That deliverance from sin does not imply deliverance from human infirmities. (2) That neither is it inconsistent with feeling our natural appetites, or with the regular gratification of them. And, (3) That salvation from sin is not inconsistent with temptations of various kinds. And all this you have clearly and fully declared in the "Plain Account of Christian Perfection." . . .

He always gives me to see, that the fulness of the promise is every Christian's privilege; and that this and every branch of salvation is to be received now, and by faith alone. And it can only be retained by the same means, by believing every moment. We cannot rest on anything that has been done, or that may be done after. This would keep us from living a life of faith; which I conceive to be no other, than the now deriving virtue from Jesus, by which we enjoy and live to God. My soul is often on the stretch for the full enjoyment of this without interruption; nor can I discharge my conscience, without urging it upon all believers, now to come unto him "who is able to save unto the uttermost."

Immediately following this testimony Wesley subjoined this exhortation:

> City-Road, London, January 5, 1780. I earnestly desire, that all our preachers would seriously consider the preceding account. And let them not be content, never to speak against the great salvation, either in public or private; and never to discourage either by word or deed any that think they have attained it: no; but prudently encourage them to "hold fast whereunto they have attained;" and strongly and explicitly exhort all believers to "go on to perfection" yea, to expect full salvation from sin every moment, by mere grace, through simple faith. (*Lives*, 2:194)

Thus spoke John Wesley in his 77th year.

36. Thomas Rankin (1734-1810)

Thomas Rankin's testimony illustrates the importance of constantly emphasizing the need to "press on to perfection."

Rankin was one of Mr. Wesley's most valuable assistants. He testified to his experience of "the more excellent way" in these words:

> After laboring as in the fire, from the month of June to September, the Lord gave me such a discovery of his love as I never had known before. I was meeting with a few Christian friends, who were all athirst for entire holiness, and after several had prayed, I also called on the name of the "Deliverer that came out of Zion, to turn away ungodliness from Jacob." While these words were pronounced with my heart and lips, "Are we not, O Lord, the purchase of thy blood? Let us then be redeemed from all iniquity," in a moment the power of God so descended upon my soul, that I could pray no more. It was
>
> "That speechless awe which dares not move,
> And all the silent heaven of love!"

I had many times experienced the power of redeeming love, and in such a manner as I scarce know whether in the body or not. But this manifestation of the presence of my adorable Lord and Savior was such as I never had witnessed before, and no words of mine properly describe it . . . Yet, as I had no particular scripture applied, I durst not say that the blood of Christ had cleansed me from all sin . . .

In the meantime, I embraced every opportunity of meeting with those whom I observed were all in earnest for deliverance from inbred sin . . . With such I constantly associated, and their prayers and conversation were a great blessing to my soul. The Lord removed all my doubts and evil reasonings, and by his grace I knew I loved the Lord my God with all my soul, mind, and strength. In short, I was not ashamed to declare, that I assuredly knew, that the Lord Jesus had purified my heart by faith in his blood, and that I felt nothing contrary to the pure love of God. (*Lives*, 5:170-72)

37. **Richard Whatcoat** (1736-1806)

Francis Asbury, Thomas Coke, and Richard Whatcoat rank highest among those who brought Methodism to the American colonies before and after independence.

If only occasionally an earnest Christian should discover sin remaining after regeneration and subsequently find full deliverance, it would be regarded as an exception to the rule. The fact that this is so uniformly the experience of twice-born men who are determined to have all the fullness of God is one of the strongest arguments for the second blessing.

Richard Whatcoat was among the most influential pioneers of American Methodism. He was born in England in 1736, converted in 1758, and sanctified wholly in 1761. He left for America in 1784 where he labored as preacher and superintendent, and died in Delaware in 1806 "in the full assurance of faith." After conversion he wrote:

I soon found that though I was justified freely, yet I was not wholly sanctified. This brought me into deep concern, and confirmed my resolution, to admit of no peace, no, nor truce, with the evils which I still found in my heart. I was sensible both that they hindered me at present in all my holy exercises, and that I could not enter into the joy of my Lord, unless they were all rooted out. These considerations led me to consider more attentively the exceeding great and precious promise, whereby we may escape all the corruption that is in the world, and be made partakers of the Divine nature.

I was much confirmed in my hope of their accomplishment, by frequently hearing Mr. Mather speak upon the subject. I saw it was the mere gift of God; and, consequently, to be received by faith. And after many sharp and painful conflicts, and many gracious visitations, on March 28th, 1761, my spirit was drawn out and engaged in wrestling with God for about two hours, in a manner I never did before. Suddenly I was stripped of all but love. I was all love, and prayer, and praise; and in this happy state, rejoicing evermore, and in everything giving thanks, I continued for some years; wanting nothing for soul or body, more than I received from day to day.

Immediately he became concerned for others and was soon preaching the gospel. The fruit of the Spirit ensuing from any crisis in spiritual experience is one of the important factors in testing its authenticity.

38. Robert Wilkinson (d. 1781)

Few of us appreciate fully the significance and importance of faith. It is to Wesley's everlasting credit that he discerned and proclaimed that one may be sanctified as well as justified by simple faith in Christ. Following the experience of sanctification, faith and obedience continue to be the condition of victory. The importance of faith is well illustrated in the experience of Robert Wilkinson. He thus described his entrance into "full redemption":

> The preacher earnestly exhorted all present to look for the second blessing, and insisted that it might be received. "No," thought I, "if there is such a thing, none can stand in more need of it than I do." But the enemy suggested, "There are those that have known God several years, and have not attained; and shalt thou be delivered who hast been justified only a few months?" Immediately I found power to resist the temptation, and said within myself, "God is not tied to time." No sooner did that thought pass through my heart, than the power of God seized me. I found I could not resist, and therefore turned myself over upon the mercy seat; I cannot express how I was. I found such a travail in my soul, as if it would burst from the body.
>
> I continued so, till I was motionless and insensible for a season. But as I was coming to myself I found such an emptying, and then such a heaven of love springing up in my soul, as I had never felt before; with an application of these blessed words, "He that believeth on me, as the Scripture hath said, out of his belly shall flow rivers of living water."

Best of all, preacher Wilkinson's life thereafter adorned the gospel in all things. Expectancy and eagerness brought the blessing in this case, as in so many others.

39. George Story (1738-1818)

One sometimes hears reports of those who, after experiencing entire sanctification, feel no more evil uprisings in their hearts for years. Often this is not so, and then doubt and discouragement follow. One feels either that he never had the experience or that he has forfeited it. It is as important to *keep* sanctified as it is to *get* sanctified. The experience of an early Methodist preacher, George Story, is instructive. Says he:

My mind had been so intensely engaged in seeking pardon, that I had quite forgot there was a further work of grace to be wrought in me. But the Lord did not suffer me to remain long under that mistake: He soon discovered the remains of the carnal mind, and the necessity of its removal. . . . I was then one evening meeting my band, when the power of the Lord descended in an uncommon manner, and I believed he had purified my heart. At first I rejected it through a sense of my unworthiness: but the witness again returned. . . . The next morning I awoke in such power and peace as I had never known; and the promises in the latter part of the thirtieth chapter of Ezekiel were applied in such a manner as left no doubt but the Lord wrought that great change in me.

Nevertheless it was not in the manner I expected. I supposed a soul saved from all sin would be a great, wise, and glorious creature; whereas I found myself infinitely little, and mean, and base: I had such a discovery of my own nothingness, as humbled me to the dust continually. I felt myself as ignorant and helpless as an infant, and knew I could not stand a moment without the Divine aid. Nor did I find such overflowing joys as I expected, but only an even permanent peace, which kept my heart in the knowledge and love of God . . .

I walked in this liberty some months, till one day I met with a circumstance which grieved me. I attended too much to the temptation, and was not inwardly watchful; so, before I was aware, the temptation took place in my heart, and I found myself angry for a moment or two. As I never expected to feel this evil any more, my distress was inconceivable for three or four hours; the enemy suggesting that I was now an apostate from the pure love of God, and could never be restored. I cried mightily to the Lord, and he discovered the device of the enemy, and healed the wound that had been made. He likewise showed me that as I had received Christ Jesus, so I must walk in him; that the same faith by which I entered into rest must be continued, in order to be established in that liberty.

70

For those who may have succumbed to temptation and fallen into sin subsequent to the experience of entire sanctification, is there any better way for recovering spiritual victory and continuing therein than indicated by George Story two centuries ago?

40. Richard Rodda (1743-1815)

A combination of sound doctrine and genuine experience is important for the promotion of holiness, as Rodda's witness attests.

One of Wesley's preachers, Mr. Richard Rodda, wrote of his testimony to full salvation as follows:

> The doctrine of Christian perfection was now preached among us, and numbers professed they had attained the blessing. I had not the least doubt of the testimony of several, as their whole behaviour agreed with their profession. I believed the doctrine, and my soul longed to experience it. I prayed that every thought and desire might center in God. While my eldest brother and I were pouring out our souls to God for this blessing, the Lord poured out his Spirit upon us; every heart present appeared like melting wax before the fire; and in that hour, God gave my mother a testimony that he had cleansed her from all unrighteousness; which I trust she retains to this day.

> My soul was now on full stretch after the blessing. I not only believed it attainable, but that I should attain it: therefore I constantly expected that Christ would come to cleanse and keep my heart. Accordingly, one Saturday night, I came to the class, and resolved not to depart till mine eyes had seen this great salvation. After I had entered the room, my heart seemed as hard as a stone; but I was not discouraged. All my prayer was, "Lord, create in me a clean heart, and renew in me a right spirit." The mighty power of God descended upon me; my heart was emptied of every evil, and Jesus took up all the room. I could no longer

71

refrain from telling what God had done for my soul. My heart was filled with love and joy, and my lips praised him. (*Lives*, 2:303)

41. **Bathsheba Hall** (b. 1745)

Often, it seems, there is a correlation between the degree over the anguish concerning indwelling sin and joy at deliverance. Mrs. Hall is a case in point.

In the *Arminian Magazine* is the following excerpt from the diary of Mrs. Bathsheba Hall, who was born in 1745. The account was published in 1781. She wrote:

> Twelve months after I found peace I saw a greater salvation to be attained. A friend gave me a clear and full account of what she experienced. God applied it strongly to my heart, and beamed forth on my soul in a wonderful manner. He now began to break up the fallow ground and shew me the mazes of sin in my heart. The more I approached the Lord in secret the more the iniquity of sin was discovered.
>
> My mind was in a violent emotion, such as were separated by these words, "I will; be thou clean." But still there was a fear of being deceived: till as soon as I rose on Sunday morning, I heard the voice of my beloved saying, "Thou art all fair; there is no spot in thee." I then felt nothing rapturous but a holy joy and solid peace, such as I expect to feel in Glory. Later, as we bowed before the Lord, our portion was, "Let there be light in our dwellings." In that moment the Lord came as a rushing mighty wind, which filled all the room. So great was the glory of the Lord we could not utter a word. Immediately I felt that I was sealed with the Holy Spirit of Promise.

This testimony has a certain self-authenticating quality. There is no morbidity, but rather a wholesome sense of soundness.

42. Francis Asbury (1745-1816)

What Wesley was to Methodism in England, Francis Asbury was to Methodism in the United States. Of Asbury his companion Freeborn Garretson said, "He prayed the best and prayed the most of all the men I knew." In a *Journal* entry the apostle of American Methodism boiled down his spiritual history thus:

> When I was a small boy and went to school I had serious thoughts, and a particular sense of the being of a God, and greatly feared both an oath and a lie. At twelve years of age the Spirit of God strove frequently and powerfully with me, but, being deprived of proper means and exposed to bad company, no effectual impressions were left on my mind . . . When between thirteen and fourteen years of age the Lord graciously visited my soul again. I then found myself more inclined to obey, and carefully attended preaching in West Bromwick; so that I heard . . . men who preached the truth . . .
>
> The next year Mr. Mather came into those parts. I was then about fifteen; and, young as I was, the Word of God soon made deep impressions on my heart, which brought me to Jesus Christ, who graciously justified my guilty soul through faith in his precious blood, and soon showed me the excellency and necessity of holiness. About sixteen I experienced a marvelous display of the grace of God, which some might think was full of sanctification, and was indeed very happy, though in an ungodly family. At about seventeen I began to hold some public meetings, and between seventeen and eighteen began to exhort and preach. (*Heart of Asbury's Journal*, p. 70)

In old age a typical sermon outline shows his stress on full salvation. On John 8:32 he emphasized that freedom means "an entire deliverance from sin, from its guilt, power, and inbeing" (p. 677). On another occasion he said, "Real religion is real holiness, and all sensations without a strong disposition for holiness are but delusive" (p. 72). Yes, Francis Asbury was a holiness preacher!

43. **William Carvosso** (1750-1834)

An English lay preacher whose name is an important one in the parade of witnesses to full salvation was left an orphan at the age of 10 and bound as an apprentice to a farmer. His mother had given him some instructions in reading, but he was unable to write until he was 65 years of age. As a boy he indulged in the pastimes of the day— cockfighting, wrestling, card playing, and other types of mischief and often of wickedness. He was 21 years of age when as a result of his sister's words and prayers he was convicted of sin. The evil one tempted him by saying that he had sinned too much and that he had passed the day of grace. He resolved that he would continue to credit God for mercy even if he were never saved; immediately, in his words, "Christ appeared within; and God pardoned all my sins, and set my soul at liberty. The Spirit himself now bore witness with my spirit that I was a child of God." (W. E. Boardman, *The Higher Christian Life* [Boston: 1871], p. 73)

Converted thus at 21 years of age, his life subsequently was a joyous one. Sometime later, however, in spite of the clear joyous sense of conversion, he discovered that he needed a deeper work of grace. In his own pictorial language he says,

> My heart appeared to me as a small garden with a large stump in it, which had been recently cut down to a level with the ground, and a little loose dirt strewn over it. Seeing something shooting up I did not like, and on attempting to pluck it up, I discovered the deadly remains of the carnal mind; and what a work must be done before I could be "meet for the Master's

use." . . . What I wanted now was inward holiness.
(p. 74)

As this concern increasingly troubled him, about a year after his clear conversion experience, tormented by his own unholiness, he turned aside into a lowly barn, there to wrestle with God. This was helpful, but he was not delivered. Later in a prayer meeting the experience that he sought came:

> I felt that I was nothing, and Christ was all in all. Him I now cheerfully received and all his offices, my prophet to teach me, my priest to atone for me, my king to reign over me. O what boundless happiness there is in Christ and all for such a poor sinner as I am. This took place on March 13, 1772. (p. 74)

This was the beginning of a life of soul winning. After his marriage he became a fisherman but was more interested in fishing for men than for fish. As a result of his evangelism among fishermen, he met regularly with them in a fisherman's hut; later in a fish-drying cellar. Then as the crowd increased, they met in a large upper room and later built a fine chapel. The whole area was transformed. He turned from fishing to farming but continued to win souls. He was a class leader with three flourishing classes. He was summoned to evangelize elsewhere. During the day he would call from house to house and hold class meetings at night. As a result over 700 were converted to Christ.

At 65, after extraordinary effort, he learned to write. His letters and autobiography have been a means of information and blessing to thousands.

The experience of God's dealing with this dedicated layman, bereft of parents at an early age and without formal education, should challenge us who have been reared in more favorable circumstances to bring forth fruit unto holiness which has as its end everlasting life.

44. **Matthias Joyce** (1754-1814?)

Pride hinders holiness. Humility is the most elusive of virtues. Some are proud of their "humility." The best cure for pride is to look to Jesus.

One of Mr. Wesley's colaborers, Mr. Matthias Joyce, was able to "pour contempt on all his pride." He struggled for two years with doubts and inner foes. At length he prayed through. He testifies:

> One who had entered into this rest loaned me Mr. Fletcher's *Treatise on Christian Perfection*, which was made a great blessing to me, both in convincing my judgment, and quickening my soul more abundantly. The part which was chiefly blessed to me was his address to imperfect believers, who believed the doctrine of Christian perfection attainable. One night, when my little family was gone to bed, I took this book to read, and as I read I met with the following words: "If thou wilt absolutely come to Mount Zion in a triumphal chariot, or make thy entrance into the New Jerusalem upon a prancing horse, thou art likely never to come there. Leave then, all thy lordly misconceptions behind; and humbly follow thy King, who makes his entry into the typical Jerusalem meek and lowly, riding upon an ass, yea, upon a colt, the foal of an ass."
>
> And as I was at this time sensible of my pride and self-will, I said in my heart, "O, this is the way! I want him to come in his meek and lowly mind." I immediately laid down the book and went to prayer . . . While I thus poured out my heart before him, I seemed to enter into the holy of holies, by faith in the blood of the Lamb. My heart expanded to receive my holy Bridegroom, when he came, as it were, riding into my soul, in his chariot of love, with all his sanctifying grace. I could do nothing now but bless and magnify the name of the Lord for this wonderful manifestation. My only language was, "Glory, glory, glory be to God!" (*Lives*, 4:256)

45. **Hester Ann Rogers** (1756-94)

Among the most victorious witnesses to full salvation in the 18th century was the Englishwoman Mrs. Hester Ann Rogers. After clearly experiencing conversion, Mrs. Rogers continued to seek more of the grace of God. In a perceptive and sensitive manner she later describes her period of heart-searchings, doubts, fears, desires, and efforts to obtain true holiness of heart. This led to a second major crisis in her Christian life at which time she received Christ in His fullness and experienced the deliverance from indwelling sin and a perfection in love. She wrote:

> Lord, my soul is delivered of her burden. I am emptied of all. I am at thy feet, helpless, worthless, worm, but take hold of thee as my fullness! Everything that I want, thou art. Thou art wisdom, strength, love, holiness: yes, and thou art mine! I am conquered and subdued by love. Thy love sinks me into nothing: it overflows my soul. O, my Jesus, thou art all in all! In thee I behold and feel all the fullness of the Godhead mind. I am now one with God. The intercourse is open: sin, inbred sin, no longer hinders the close communion; and God is all my own. O, the depths of that solid peace my soul now felt!

Her life thereafter was a constant source of inspiration to others. She became one of the brightest lights in the firmament of early English Methodism.

While the negative phase is prominent in her writings —the emptying of sin and self—there is also strong emphasis on the filling of the Spirit and the empowering for effective service. This her life clearly demonstrated in the years that followed.

46. **William McKendree** (1757-1835)

One of the great names in the history of American Methodism is that of William McKendree, who was the first native American bishop in the Methodist church. Most of his ministerial life was spent in Tennessee, but his influence spread from the Atlantic seaboard to the Mississippi River. He was born near Richmond, Va., the eldest of eight children of a middle-class family. His formal education was slight, though he did acquire an effective command of the English language.

The McKendrees were communicants in the church. Methodism was just getting started on the seaboard where it was largely in eclipse during the Revolutionary War. When McKendree was 18 or 19 years of age, a revival broke out among the Methodists in his community. As a seeker, he united as a probationer in a Methodist class but soon gave up his profession. Years later, when McKendree was 30 and had finished his service in the army, a revival occurred in his district. Within a year 1,800 persons were converted through the ministry of Evangelist John Easter. McKendree came under deep conviction and, following a sermon by the evangelist, found

> the great deep of my heart was broken up, its desperately wicked nature was disclosed and the awfully ruinous consequences clearly appeared. My repentance was sincere . . . I ventured my all on Christ. In a moment my soul was delivered of a burden too heavy to be bourne and joy succeeded sorrow.

Soon after his conversion, McKendree "began to reach out with all eagerness of his renewed heart for this great blessing" of entire sanctification (E. E. Hoss, *William McKendree: A Biographical Study* [Nashville: 1916], p. 31). As McKendree hungered and thirsted for full salvation, groaning after it day and night, he said,

The more I sought the blessing of sanctification, the more I felt the need of it. . . . One morning I walked into the field, and while I was musing such an overwhelming power of the divine being overshadowed me as I had never experienced before. Unable to stand, I sank to the ground more than filled with transport. My cup ran over, and I cried aloud.

This experience, his biographer continues, "did not terminate in itself, but left an everlasting impress upon the character of McKendree, and showed itself thereafter in all manner of holiness and uprightness of conversation." The account continues:

This great baptism of the Spirit, not breaking in on him without antecedent conditions, but accompanied in answer to prayer and faith, was of tremendous significance to the young in heart Christian. He never forgot it.

Throughout his life McKendree continued to preach and profess and exemplify this perfect love which casts out all fear. He not only bore fruit, but after this pruning and purging he brought forth even more fruit.

During his youth and until he was 30 years of age, William McKendree exhibited few, if any, of the extraordinary abilities he later manifested. Following his conversion, and especially after his entire sanctification, he became an extraordinary personality. It is illustrative of the fact that it is not so much the vessel as the One who controls the vessel that determines its effectiveness.

47. **William Adams** (1759-?)

When Methodism was most vigorous, the doctrine of sanctification was kept in prominence.

William Adams was an effective preacher in American Methodism in the latter half of the 18th century. Born in

Virginia in 1759, he was converted in 1775 and called to preach. Meanwhile

> the Lord convinced him more deeply of the inward corruption of his heart. He was now all athirst for a heart perfectly devoted to God; crying out,
>
>> "'Tis worse than death my God to love,
>> And not my God alone."
>
> And on the 17th of August . . . he believed the Lord had saved him from all his inbred sin; and felt what he could not fully express. For some time he had no doubt of this work being wrought in him; and, indeed, none who knew him could disbelieve him; for the tree was known for its fruit. But the enemy of souls soon robbed him in a measure of his confidence respecting this work, so that he came short of his gracious privilege.

Later he served the Baltimore circuit where he found "not a few who could testify that the blood of Christ had cleansed them from all unrighteousness." As a result "he soon found the work of God reviving in his soul" and became established in grace, having a "constant sense of the indwelling Spirit of God." At a quarterly meeting he declared

> that the Lord had taken away every doubt of his being perfected in love; and had given him a confidence which was stronger than death and all the powers of darkness. He well knew the happiness and advantages of conversing with such Christians as had experienced a deliverance from indwelling sin, and were daily pressing after a growth in grace.

This illustrates how Spirit-filled laymen can help their preacher to become established in the "fullness of the blessing." (*Lives,* 6:277)

48. **William Black** (1760-1834)

In healthy-minded souls the normal sequence of spiritual development is a concern for one's own full salvation and then a concern for the salvation of others. This is well illustrated in the life of an early superintendent in American Methodism, William Black. After his conversion he wrote:

> When I first set out in the ways of God, I thought if I was once converted, I should never feel the least evil desire, wandering of thought from God, or aversion to duty. I concluded, sin will be all destroyed, and I shall know it no more. But how mistaken! I found my conflicts were just beginning; or myself but newly entered on the field of battle. O, what a depth of wickedness I found still in my heart; What a den of thieves, a cage of unclean birds, a nest of corruption, pride, self, unbelief, love of the world, aversion to duty! All loathsome to behold, and contrary to the will of that God whom in my soul I loved.
>
> Yet, blessed be God, they had not the dominion over me. The moment they were discovered, my soul rose in indignation against them, fled to the atoning blood, and looked to heaven for deliverance. I hated, I abhorred them as the spawn of hell; so that they did not break my peace. I still held fast the beginning of my confidence, and felt the Spirit of the Lord bearing witness with my spirit that I was a child of God. But a view of these things greatly humbled me, and showed me the continual need I had of Jesus Christ. It sent me often to Calvary with this cry,
>
> > "Every moment, Lord, I need
> > The merit of Thy death!"

He found victory, apparently, not in a second crisis but rather in a moment-by-moment appeal to Christ for cleansing in His blood. His life was henceforth characterized by great blessing in prayer, great concern for the souls of others, and great effectiveness in preaching the gospel.

49. M. Martindale (fl. 1791)

In this, as in similar witnesses, a sense of deliverance and purity does not arise from a mild view of sin. Instead, an awareness of sin's enormity leads to the cry for an experience of cleansing.

The experience of M. Martindale appears in the February, 1797, issue of the *Arminian Magazine,* published by John Wesley:

> I believe he never saved a viler sinner than myself . . . The Lord . . . gave me to see the necessity of sanctification. I read, fasted and prayed, and used all the means of grace, in order to obtain this blessing. I was convinced that it could only be received by faith . . . I understood that although the work is gradual, there must be a last moment, wherein sin ceases to exist in the human heart; and when grace begins to reign triumphant over all the powers of body, soul, and spirit. The more I struggled . . . the more I saw and felt my exceeding sinfulness. Never until now had I fully realized the depth of iniquity which lurked in my fallen nature . . . For hours together have I wrestled with God in earnest prayer for sanctification.
>
> One morning, when in an agony of prayer, I was enabled to believe unto full salvation, I felt the pure love of God filling all my soul, and captivating all my thoughts and desires. To the best of my judgment I walked in this blessed state for more than eighteen months; in which I found neither anger, pride, fear, nor any of those uneasy and sinful tempers, so contrary to pure love . . . I was not exempt from temptations but they had no power to harm me.

Again we see the ancient promise verified, "Ye shall seek me, and find me, when ye shall search for me with all your heart" (Jer. 29:13).

50. **Jane Kerr** (c. 1795)

After reading numerous testimonies to full salvation, one is impressed with the variety of ways of describing the experience and at the same time with the essential agreement of the witnesses. Amid variety in incidentals there is unity in essentials. This basic similarity among different witnesses argues for the reality and distinctiveness of the second work of grace. In the following testimony there is discernible the basic pattern of a child of God being awakened to a deeper spiritual need and finding rest through faith. This is the experience of Mrs. Jane Kerr.

> As she retained her first love, and unreservedly devoted herself to the Lord, he did not permit her to remain long without a discovery of the nature and necessity of a deeper work of grace; she saw the remains of the carnal mind, and the happiness those enjoy who are pure in heart . . . The enemy suggested that the small degree of faith and love that she possessed, rendered her unfit to obtain the blessing of complete sanctification. At another time he insinuated that it was quite too soon for her to expect purity of heart, because many professors who had been much longer on the way had not yet obtained it.
>
> At the quarterly meeting, while Mr. T. H. was at prayer before the first sermon, the Lord granted her the blessing she so ardently desired; he spoke in great love and mighty power to her soul, "I will, be thou clean." Immediately she was conscious that the virtue of the blood of Christ was applied to her heart in such a manner, as to remove inward sin, with all hereditary evil and unhappy tempers that are connected with it . . . Her grateful heart overflowed with love, and her lips showed forth his praise. (*Arminian*, April, 1795)

Like many others, Mrs. Kerr was tempted to doubt that the blessing was for her. She believed and obeyed, hence her joy.

51. A Typical Witness of The Way (1779)

In John Wesley's *Arminian Magazine* for the year 1779 this testimony to full salvation appeared, typical of many others.

One of them, speaking of the wickedness of his heart, I was greatly surprised; telling them, I felt no such thing, my heart being kept in peace and love all day long. But it was not a week before I felt the swelling of pride, and the storms of anger and self-will . . . We prayed for each other, and believed that God was both willing and able to purify our hearts from all sin.

This summer . . . a great outpouring of the Spirit [occurred] in London and many were athirst for the whole Christian salvation. So was I—I loved the very name of it . . . I loved the people in pursuit of it . . . I was convinced more deeply than ever of inbred sin . . . After dinner in prayer I was baptized with the Holy Ghost and fire, and felt nothing but love and desired nothing but more love without intermission.

As testimonies to entire sanctification multiplied, it became evident that the usual sequence was forgiveness of sin, joy in the Lord, awareness of remaining depravity, confession of indwelling sin, and prayer for complete cleansing, and finally a complete emptying of carnal traits and a complete filling of divine love and power in response to faith in Christ. The remarkable discovery then made and set forth more specifically than ever before—since New Testament times—was (1) that sin remains in the believer; (2) that complete deliverance is a present possibility; and (3) that this deliverance may come instantly as soon as confession, consecration, and faith are exercised.

Nineteenth-Century Witnesses

52. Thomas Chalmers (1780-1847)

This Scottish preacher is best known to ministerial students as the author of a sermon entitled "The Expulsive Power of a New Affection." Here Chalmers calls for an uncompromising break with sin.

> Sin is that scandal which must be rooted out from the great spiritual household over which the Divinity rejoices. Strange administration indeed, for sin to be so hateful to God as to lay all who had incurred it under death, and yet, when readmitted into life, that sin should be permitted and that what was before the object of destroying vengeance should now become the object of an upheld and protected toleration. Now that the penalty is taken off, think you it is possible that the unchangeable God has so given up his antipathy to sin as that man, ruined and redeemed man, may now perseveringly indulge under the new arrangement, in that which under the old destroyed him?
>
> . . . I now breathe the air of loving-kindness from Heaven, and can walk before God in peace and graciousness; shall I again attempt the incompatible alliance of two principles so adverse as that of an approving God and a persevering sinner? How shall we, recovered from so awful a catastrophe, continue that which involved us in it? The cross of Christ by the same mighty and decisive stroke wherewith it moved the curse of sin away from us, also surely moves away the power and the love of it from us.

In short, we may look for redemption from the power as well as the guilt of sin. Praise the Lord!

53. Charles G. Finney (1792-1875)

Charles G. Finney is esteemed as one of the most effective revivalists of all time. He was also a pioneer theologian and social reformer. We can learn much from him.

The religious experience of Finney is as unique as it was striking. In it can be discerned two distinct phases: a sense of pardon and peace, and later the baptism with the Holy Spirit and fullness of joy. After laboring under a load of sin, he suddenly felt no more guilt. "All sense of sin, all consciousness of present sin or guilt, had departed from me." "I was so quiet and peaceful," he continues, "that I tried to feel concerned about that, lest it should be a result of my having grieved the Spirit away." At this time Finney was unlearned in the Bible or in theology. A few hours later, after a precious season of prayer, he says:

> As I turned and was about to take a seat by the fire, I received a mighty baptism of the Holy Ghost. Without any expectation of it, without ever having the thought in my mind that there was any such thing for me, without any recollection that I had ever heard the thing mentioned by any person in the world, the Holy Spirit descended upon me in a manner that seemed to go through me, body and soul. I could feel the impression, like a wave of electricity, going through and through me. Indeed it seemed to come in waves and waves of liquid love; for I could not express it in any other way. It seemed like the very breath of God. I can recollect distinctly that it seemed to fan me, like immense wings.
>
> No words can express the wonderful love that was shed abroad in my heart. I wept aloud with joy and love; and I do not know but I should say, I literally bellowed out the unutterable gushings of my heart. These waves came over me, and over me, and over me, one after the other, until I recollect I cried out, "I shall die if these waves continue to pass over me." I said, "Lord, I cannot bear any more;" yet I had no fear of death.

For days after this his soul was aflood with love, and with great power he gave witness to the grace of the Lord Jesus. Every study of the holiness movement in America must recognize the beneficent influence of Finney.

54. Leonidas L. Hamline (1797-1865)

Toward the middle of the 19th century many leaders of the Methodist church in the United States became increasingly explicit and emphatic concerning the necessity of entire sanctification. Prominent among these was Bishop Leonidas L. Hamline. His biographer, W. C. Palmer, states that in 1842 he became acutely aware of his need of heart purity. He realized that there were "roots" of many evils within which were checked under the reign of grace, "yet were ever ready to spring up under the least declining of faith and love." He wrestled in prayer for days. He came to love holiness, so that he desired it, "not only for safety, but for its own sake." In his quest, he read not only the Bible but such writers as Wesley, Fletcher, Watson, Benson, Merritt, and Mahan.

After hearing a sermon on holiness in 1842 at New Albany, Ohio, he sought publicly for the experience. On Monday morning, in his room, he was profoundly impressed with "the image of Christ as the single object of desire." The question, "Why do you not take this image for he has taken yours?" was suggested to him. He seemed to hear the words, "Look at the crucified Lamb . . . now, just now, he freely offers you all. . . ."

All at once he felt as though a hand, not feeble but omnipotent, not of wrath but of love, were laid upon his brow. It seemed to press upon his whole being, and to diffuse through with sin-consuming energy. "Wherever it moved it seemed to leave the impress of the Saviour's image" (W. C. Palmer, *Life and Letters of Leonidas L. Hamline*, p. 101).

No longer was he haunted by the disquieting awareness of inward sin. His testimony at the Ohio Annual Conference at Chillicothe in 1843 to the fullness of divine love and purity rang out with convincing winsomeness and clarity. Thus there came to be another powerful witness and advocate of the "more excellent way."

55. Asa Mahan (1800-1889)

After a perspective of more than a century, several students of American church history have come to the conclusion that no one man was more influential in launching the modern holiness movement in this country than the former president of Oberlin College, Asa Mahan. It was his influence which led those in the Wesleyan tradition to link entire sanctification with the baptism of the Holy Spirit. This did not come through as clearly with John Wesley as it did later with John Fletcher, Adam Clarke, and Asa Mahan. It is now widely recognized in the holiness movement, whether in the Methodist tradition or in the Pentecostal tradition, that the baptism of the Spirit coincides with entire sanctification.

Dr. Mahan cites his own experience substantiating his understanding of the biblical teaching on this subject. He reports that when he was ordained as a Presbyterian minister, he soon felt his deficiency with respect of "building of believers in the most holy faith." He reports:

> Under my ministry, many were convicted, converted, and led to Christ in the matter of justification. But how after this to induce in the convert that form of the divine life which I knew to be portrayed in the New Testament, and foretold in the Old—here I felt myself "weighed in the balances and found wanting." The reason I knew to be, that want of that life perfected in my own experience, hence the subject of personal holiness became with me a central object of thought, inquiry, reading, and prayer.

His report continues,

> When alone with God, one day, in a deep forest, for example, I said distinctly and definitely to my

90

Heavenly Father, there is one thing that I desired above all else—the consciousness that my heart was pure in his sight; that if he would grant me this one blessing, I would accept any providences that might attend me. This I said, "with strong crying and tears."

In this state I came to Oberlin, as the president of that college. I had been there but a short time, when a general inquiry arose in the church after the divine secret of holy living, and a direct appeal was made to brother Finney and myself for specific instructions on the subject, which induced in me an intensity of desire, indescribable, after that secret. Just as my whole being became centered in that one desire, the cloud lifted, and I stood in the clear sunlight of the face of God. The secret was all plain to me now, and I knew, also, how to lead inquirers into the King's highway.

Since that good hour, my sun has not gone down, neither has my moon withdrawn itself. Christ, reader, will never write his new name and give you that "new white stone which no man knoweth but him that receiveth it" until you come to value above all Christ a possession of his moral image and likeness, and until you seek that image and likeness with immutable fixedness of desire and purpose. "Then shall ye seek me and find me, when you shall search for me with all your heart." (Asa Mahan, *The Baptism of the Holy Ghost* [1870], pp. 107-9)

56. Benjamin Hackney (b. 1805)

In the early days of the modern holiness movement the stress was upon faith and "the instantaneous blessing" in contrast to the older view that holiness was obtained gradually.

This happened at a camp meeting for the promotion of holiness at Aurora, Ill., about 1860:

Among the rest who attended this meeting was the Hon. Benjamin Hackney, of Aurora. He had been converted but a short time, and under the preaching of Father Coleman, had come to see the doctrine of holiness clearly, but had not yet entered into the experience. Sunday evening, just before the preaching service, he was walking back and forth across the grounds in meditation, when he met Father Coleman, and said, "Father Coleman, I've got everything upon the altar; what shall I do next?" "Oh, just leave it there," said the old veteran, and passed on.

. . . Mr. Hackney resumed his walk, and his meditations. But to himself he said, "Well; that is a strange way to treat a man! Why did he not try to help me? Perhaps that is the way to do. Well, I'll do that." He continued his walk, thinking and praying and waiting upon the Lord. Little by little his faith took hold, and little by little came the peace of believing. The assurance began to spring up in his heart, and at last he was enabled to say:

> "Tis done, thou dost this moment save,
>   With full salvation bless;
> Redemption through thy blood I have,
>   And spotless love and peace."
>
> (J. G. Terrill, *Life of Redfield*, p. 410)

57. **Mr. Carpenter** (d. 1847)

A man named Carpenter died in Newark, N.J., over 100 years ago. At his funeral in the Presbyterian church some of the ministers stated publicly that it had been carefully estimated that this layman had led 10,000 souls to Christ. He was limited in education and gifts, but the factor that accounted for his influence was the baptism of the Holy Spirit. He was particularly effective in personal work.

On one occasion he with another Christian entered a stagecoach to go from Newark to New York, a distance of some 15 miles. "They found seven individuals, all impenitent, with them in the vehicle. While on the way, or very soon after, all those seven individuals were hopefully converted, and that through the influence exerted during the ride."

Shortly before his death this humble man of God told a friend that for the past 10 years he had walked "in the cloudless light of the Son of righteousness." During this period, he related, he had experienced entire sanctification and had continued in that grace. He stated his conviction that "soon this doctrine would be a leading theme in the churches" (Mahan, *Baptism of the Holy Ghost*, p. 88).

The promise "Ye shall receive power, after that the Holy Ghost is come upon you: and ye shall be witnesses" is true of laymen as well as ministers of the gospel. A great emphasis upon the doctrine and experience of entire sanctification would result in a great tide of revival in which sinners would be converted. It is significant today that the most rapidly growing denominations in Christendom are those which lay most stress upon the Spirit-filled life. There is vitality in this doctrine and experience!

58. **Sarah Lankford** (1806-96)

The modern holiness movement owes much to the women who pioneered its inception. None was more influential than two sisters, Sarah Lankford and Phoebe Palmer.

The "Tuesday Meeting" sponsored by Phoebe Palmer and her husband was a blessing to thousands for a period of over 50 years. These holiness meetings were originated by Mrs. Palmer's sister, Mrs. Sarah A. Lankford, in 1836. Her testimony is very clear and positive:

> In my fifteenth year my class-leader presented me with Wesley's *Plain Account of Christian Perfection.* I began to pray earnestly for all that was my privilege to enjoy. My desires were intense, temptations powerful, but oh, how often in flying to Jesus for refuge, have I felt all the sweetness and security of a babe in its mother's arms.

My views were not clear, but I wanted something. A camp meeting came, and I said, "I will get the blessing there." On Monday, at the first meeting, seekers were invited forward for prayers. I presented myself as seeking a clean heart. All the week, at every meeting, I was found at the mourner's bench, praying and struggling. The last night of the camp meeting I was not satisfied. The whole night was spent in tears, with unutterable groaning. Often was heard by me, "The blood of Jesus Christ cleanseth from all sin,"—only believe. My heart as often replied, "I do believe, but I want to feel."

Dear ones remained with me. The day was dawning, but I said, I cannot give it up, I must be blessed. My dear mother whispered, "You must leave this place." She put loving arms around me, gently raising me to my feet. Finding I could struggle no longer, I consented to believe, and as I said, "Lord, I will believe, the blood of Jesus cleanseth," my swollen eyes met the first crimson ray in the east; the joyous transition of that moment cannot be described. My heart and my voice exclaimed Glory! The Son of Righteousness has risen with healing in his wings.

After being wholly sanctified at the age of 15, she was not encouraged at the class meeting and finally lost her testimony. For a time she was in despondency, then began again to seek the Lord. She says:

Up to this time I had not had very clear or painful views of the natural depravity of the human heart. It was not until 1824 the veil was lifted, that I might glance at the corruptions of my nature. Almost overwhelmed at the sight, and while abhorring myself, I was astonished that even the infinite love of Jesus could look on one so impure. My views of sin, its awful demerit, and anguish felt in consequence, was now much, much more clear and keen, than before justification . . .

In the early part of 1825 I obtained the *Christian Manual,* by Rev. Timothy Merritt, and through this means was led to expect deliverance through faith in the atonement . . .

One Saturday evening I resolved not to rise from my knees the whole night, or even the next day, without the witness of purity. I pled earnestly. Several times the promise was presented, "The blood of Jesus cleanseth." Tremblingly faith would take hold and say, I do believe! but impatient for further manifestations, I would resume pleading. About one o'clock in the morning, I opened the precious Bible on "Ye have need of patience, that, after ye have done the will of God, ye might receive the promise. For yet a little while, and he that shall come will come, and will not tarry. Now the just shall live by faith." I felt the reproof; also the encouragement; and calmly said, "Lord, I will believe; I am wholly thine; help me to abide in thee." I then retired, resolving to live by faith.

The next day the Spirit reaffirmed this promise to her, and henceforth hers was a life of continued victory and fruitful service.

59. C. K. True (1809-78)

One of the most distinctive elements in the theology of John Wesley was the witness of the Spirit. To most of Wesley's contemporaries this was regarded as exceedingly presumptuous. The bishop of London is quoted as saying, "This is a very horrid thing." It exposed Wesley to the charge of fanaticism or "enthusiasm." It was Wesley who called the attention of the Christian Church to the witness of the Spirit, not so much to the truth of the Scriptures as did Calvinism, as to the Spirit's witness to one's acceptance "in the beloved." Wesley emphasized that God gives the witness of the Spirit both to one's conversion from sin and also to one's entire sanctification or heart purity. This witness of the Spirit finds its scriptural basis in the eighth chapter of Romans and the First Epistle of John.

It is also borne out in a multitude of witnesses, among

which is Dr. C. K. True. In a sermon preached at Eastham Camp Meeting, August 11, 1848, he said:

> You need not be afraid to believe that you receive while you pray; for according to the testimony of thousands you thereupon receive the direct witness of the Spirit. This is what you had hoped to receive first in order to believe; but it comes, if it comes at all, as the confirmation of your faith.
>
> One aged brother . . . told us for forty years he had been seeking holiness of heart but had never received the witness until he received it at this camp meeting. But while in secret prayer, in the retirement of the woods, he received the witness of the Spirit.

Now with reference to his own experience True continued,

> But I had received no special witness of the Spirit. I had confessed and abjured all my sins; I had renewed my consecration to God; I had cast myself upon the atonement; I had pled the promises, . . . and I had resolved to believe that my prayer was answered, and not to doubt until I had evidence to the contrary. . . . The day before the meeting was dissolved I retired as usual into the woods, and laid the whole matter before God, and told him all that was in my heart. While prostrate before him in consecration and prayer, what seemed a heavenly glory pervaded my soul and thrilled my body, accompanied by a sense of union with God in affection and love. It seemed very distinct from any excitement in my own mind, and I felt it was the Spirit of God bearing witness with my spirit.

This is in clear agreement with Wesley's teaching on the subject. In Wesley's words, "It is a divine evidence and conviction that He is able and willing to sanctify us now; there needs to be added one thing more—a divine evidence and conviction that He *doeth it.*" (W. McDonald, *The New Standard of Piety*, pp. 197-205)

60. John Wesley Redfield (1810-63)

One of the eloquent and effective evangelists of the middle 19th century was Dr. John Wesley Redfield of the Methodist Episcopal church, and later of the Free Methodist church. As a result of his own experience he was a staunch advocate of the doctrine and experience of holiness. For months and years he sought earnestly but in vain, because he did not seek by faith; instead he thought that his success in seeking would be in proportion to his exertion. At a camp meeting Dr. and Mrs. Palmer instructed him in the way of God more perfectly. He wrote:

> I then saw the way of faith as never before, and I said to myself, "I have tried everything else but faith; I will now go out and make an experiment." I saw that everything I hoped for, feared and desired was now, with all that I expected in the world to come, all, all to be staked on a single act, to be lost or won forever.
>
> I offered this prayer, "O Lord, thou knowest all hearts, and that I want to do thy will. I have tried honestly to know all, and to do all I could to get right, and thou knowest that I stand ready to do or to suffer anything imposed upon me by which to secure the great blessing of perfect love. I have tried everything but this single and apparently inefficient and hopeless act of faith, which looks to my reason more like presumption than like an act that can do me any good; and now, O Lord, seeing no other untried way, I will make the venture, and if it fails, on thee must rest the responsibility. If I am lost for believing in Christ, I cannot help it."

He then made the leap of faith, received the assurance of cleansing, was tempted repeatedly to doubt, made the leap repeatedly, and soon was established in perfect love. Significant is his statement of "the philosophy of faith":

> I breathe but one breath of air at a time; that is all I need; when I want another, it will be allowed. So I do not need a stock of the joys of salvation for future

97

use, but take it, breathe it, by acts of faith just as I have need. Continuously acting faith brings a continuous supply. (J. G. Terrill, *Life of Redfield,* pp. 90-99)

61. **Henry Ward Beecher** (1813-87)

Endorsements of "perfect love" are especially welcome from those outside of the Wesleyan-Pietistic tradition. Beecher held one of the most influential pulpits of his day, a day in which pulpits were influential. He was brother of the woman who, in Lincoln's words, "started the Civil War," Harriet Beecher Stowe (author of *Uncle Tom's Cabin*).

During the latter half of the 19th century there was perhaps a greater concern with the experience of evangelical holiness than at any other time in Christian history since New Testament times. It is evidenced in part by the founding of the National Association for the Promotion of Holiness and the organization of the Keswick conventions. Reflecting the spirit of the times are the words of the influential pastor of Plymouth (Congregational) Church in Brooklyn, Henry Ward Beecher. Speaking of the "higher life," he remarked:

> The most stupid of all heresies is that of poking through the world, munching life, as an ox munches grass, with the head eternally down to the earth, in a coarse, vulgar experience—"the practical, common-sense life," as it is called. Men by thousands, by swarming millions, live in that unproductive life, and nobody thinks there is any danger in it; but when there is one who undertakes to break away from that degraded life and go up into a higher state, men say, "There is danger of enthusiasm."
>
> What if, out of every five who seek this higher life, four fail? The success of the one is worth the endeavor. Because there are counterfeiters, we are not to throw away good money. There could not be any counterfeits if there were not good money . . . There is

98

such an experience; . . . I would teach it and preach it;
for that way lies the development of human experience,
human life, human character.

If, then, any of you are seeking, with some doubt,
this hidden life, if any of you are looking wistfully in
the direction of the higher Christian experience, oh, my
brother, oh, my sister, do not be discouraged. Open
wide the door and say, "Come in, Lord Jesus. Spirit of
promise, enter. Cleanse me, and dwell with me." For,
of all the blessings of this life, and of all the blessedness
of the life to come, there is none comparable with that
which shall be yours when God pours his own happiness
and peace into the full-urned souls of those who seek to
trust him and love him.

62. **Benjamin Titus Roberts** (1823-93)

Roberts was an evangelistic pastor in the Genesee
Conference of the Methodist church before being expelled
on charges of "insubordination."

Like many other young ministers, Rev. B. T. Roberts,
a founder of the Free Methodist church, discovered the
need of heart holiness after a clear conversion and call to
the ministry. Of the camp meeting at Collins, N.Y. (Genesee Conference, M.E. church, 1850), he wrote:

> The subject of holiness received special attention
> . . . Two paths were distinctly marked out before me. I
> saw that I might be a popular preacher, gain applause,
> do but little good in reality, and at last lose my soul; or,
> I saw that I might take the narrow way, declare the
> whole truth as it is in Jesus, meet with persecution and
> opposition, but see a thorough work of grace go on and
> gain heaven. Grace was given to make a better choice.
> I deliberately gave myself anew to the Lord, to declare
> the whole truth as it is in Jesus, and to take the
> narrow way.
>
> The blessing came. The Spirit fell upon me in an
> overwhelming degree. I received a power to labor such
> as I had never possessed before. This consecration has

never been taken back. I have many times had to humble myself before the Lord for having grieved his Spirit. I have been but an unprofitable servant. It is by grace alone that I am saved. Yet the determination is fixed to obey the Lord and take the narrow way, come what will. (B. H. Roberts, *Benjamin Titus Roberts*, pp. 50 f.)

The keynote of Roberts' experience was consecration. It reminds one of Wesley's opinion that two alternatives lie before each Christian, the high way of complete consecration and the low way. In Roberts' case, the consecration once made, a life of continued victory was possible conditioned on a continued consecration and obedience. So it is with all of us.

63. **Daniel Steele** (1824-1914)

Daniel Steele was a Methodist minister and also professor at Boston University School of Theology. There he held nearly every position including that of dean. His competence in the language of the New Testament is still recognized. It was he who was selected to write the article on entire sanctification in the *International Standard Bible Encyclopedia*. His testimony to the infilling of the Holy Spirit is as follows, though considerably abbreviated by this editor.

Steele, a Methodist minister for 20 years, explained that his two decades of ministry were "almost fruitless in conversions, through a lack of unction from the Holy One. My great error was in depending on the truth alone to break stony hearts. The Holy Spirit, though formally acknowledged and invoked, was practically ignored." After hearing an evangelist with "extraordinary power to awaken slumbering professors," he discovered that the secret of the evangelist's spiritual power was in the fullness of the Holy Spirit "enjoyed as an abiding blessing, styled by him, 'rest in Jesus.'" Steele sought earnestly this gift of the Holy Spirit but found it necessary to make a public confession of his sin "in preaching self more than Christ." He was led to seek the presence of the Comforter in his heart and concluded, on the basis of Scripture, that "the Comforter is for me now." As he meditated on the great facts of Christ's life and His promise to send the Holy Spirit, he reported,

> . . . suddenly I became conscious of a mysterious power exerting itself upon my sensibilities . . . like electric sparks passing through my bosom with slight but painless shocks, melting my hard heart into a fiery stream of love. Christ became so unspeakably precious, that I instantly dropped all good . . . everything, in the twinkling of an eye.

As he cried out for nothing but Christ, he experienced the love of God shed abroad in his heart by the Holy Spirit.

> . . . it seemed as the attraction to Jesus, the loadstone of my soul, was so strong that it would be drawn out of my body, and through the college window by which I was sitting, and upward into the sky. O, how vivid and real was all this to me! I was more certain that Christ loved me than I was of the existence of the solid earth and the shining sun. I intuitively apprehended Christ. . . . The joy for weeks was unspeakable. The impulse was irresistible to speak to everybody, saint or sinner, Protestant or Papist, in public and in private. . . .
>
> I can no longer accuse myself of unbelief, the root of all sin . . . if sin consists only in active energies, I am not conscious of such dwelling within me. If sin consists in a state, as some assert, I infer that I am not in such a state, from the absence of central energies flowing therefrom, and more specially from the indwelling of the Holy Spirit.

Steele continues,

> . . . the doctrine of entire sanctification, as a specialty, had not been my hobby, but rather my ab-

101

horrence, in consequence of the imperfect manner in which it has been inculcated and exemplified. Hence, if there is anything in this experience confirmatory of that doctrine as a distinct work, concerning my former attitude toward this subject, my testimony is something like that of Saul of Tarsus to the truth of Christianity. If I have any advice to give to Methodists, it is to cease to discuss the subtleties and endless questions arising from entire sanctification or Christian perfection, and all cry mightily to God for the baptism of the Holy Spirit. This is certainly promised to all believers in Jesus. Methodism, thus appointed to the pulpit and pew, will be the mightiest Christian power in our country and in the world. (W. McDonald, *The New Testament Standard of Piety* [Christian Witness Co., 1882], pp. 275-82)

His book *Milestone Papers* is one of his most valuable heritages. He speaks of the "milestone," the anniversary of his entering into the experience of perfect love. Much of it reads like the *Confessions* of Augustine or John Wesley's *Journal*. Five years after his "Beulah Land experience," he writes,

It is the seventeenth of November the anniversary of the spiritual manifestation of Jesus Christ to me as the perfect Savior from all sin—an event transcending all others in my sojourn on earth. To the salvation wrought on that day so long as I can move tongue or pen I must testify. Rather, I *will* testify.

O, Lord Jesus, how often during these five wonderful years have I wearied an unbelieving world and half-believing church with my attestation of thy marvelous power to save. But all my utterances fail to express the greatness and blessedness of my glorious deliverance. I cannot express in thought, much less in words, the immensity of thy love, an ocean without bottom or brim. I cannot tell the story, and I cannot let it alone. By thy grace, blessed Holy Ghost and abiding Comforter, I will not cease the attempt.

In many cases of the deeper spiritual life there is a second crisis subsequent to conversion but little reported spiritual progress after that. Many times a sort of a plateau is reached with the stress being on the crises in the past, not process in the present. But with Steele, his jubilation continued unabated.

Steele continued to assess his present relation to Christ as including

> first, salvation from doubt; second, the death of personal ambition; third, perfect rest from all apprehension of future ill; fourth, oneness with Christ; fifth, faith as a steady living principle; sixth, love has been a well of water within springing up to everlasting life, instead of an intermittent brook ice bound in winter and dried up in mid summer and seventh, peace, the legacy of Jesus changest not.

These, Steele tells his readers, are the constancies in his life replacing the previous intermittencies and fragments.

Such is the testimony of one of Methodism's scholar-saints 33 years after he had become acquainted with Christ his Savior and 5 years after he received the Pentecostal baptism of the Holy Spirit. No one can read his glowing testimony without feeling the power, persuasiveness, and winsomeness of this witness of the way. In these *Milestone Papers* and his other writings, Steele being dead in the flesh yet speaks. (See Daniel Steele, *Milestone Papers* [New York: Phillips and Hunt, 1876].)

64. **M. L. Haney** (b. 1825)

This evangelist of many years' experience wrote the story of his life at the age of 79. He attributes his conversion to the influence of a Christian home. Family prayers, his father's righteousness, and his mother's prayer life left a deep and beneficent impression upon him. After years of yearning to be saved but fearful to present himself as a sinner, his conversion occurred at a watch night service when the minister in charge invited him to seek Christ. After struggling for a period, the Holy Spirit suggested the question, "Will you now obey?" He answered, "Yes, Lord, I will." Instantly "Christ came before me as my sin-pardoning Savior . . . I found myself consciously possessed of a new life which I had never had before."

He then became a Methodist preacher and, while engaged in the prescribed course of study, learned that he should seek an experience beyond that of conversion— that of perfect love. As a pastor he visited every family in his circuit. He usually arose to pray at four in the morning, and fasted twice each week. His delight was in the law of the Lord and in witnessing for Christ. He grew in grace rapidly. In retrospect he says he did not seek the experience of full salvation because he was expecting an immense gust of glory. Also he did not seek it by faith.

In the summer of 1847 at Knox County, Ill., he attended a camp meeting where he learned that several had experienced full salvation. On the last night of the camp meeting many were praying through to entire sanctification. Haney was engaged in praying both for sinners seeking forgiveness and for believers seeking the filling of the Spirit. Although he had come 100 miles to obtain the experience of holiness, he had become so preoccupied with the needs of others that he had forgotten his own quest. The Spirit whispered to him, "It is time to give attention to your own soul."

He at once began to pray, about ten o'clock at night, and prayed all night without ceasing. At daybreak he was exhausted. As he became quiet the Lord showed him the carnal nature still within him in contrast to the white light of holiness which exposed the sin. In his agony for deliverance, the Spirit said that two things were necessary: consecration and faith in Jesus. He exclaimed, "O Lord, is that all?" The Spirit continued to probe him, asking him questions about his willingness to do this or that, to which he answered, "Yes." He was questioned, "Will you be all Mine and trust My blood to cleanse you from all sin and testify to this wherever I ask you to?" To this he whole-heartedly answered, "Yes."

He now realized that his consecration was complete and he took Jesus as his complete Sanctifier. Although he felt exhausted and empty, he nevertheless testified to the work of God's grace in cleansing him from sin. Later that night while at family prayer the Holy Spirit witnessed to him that his deliverance was complete. His soul was "flooded with glory"; the witness of the Spirit turned his faith to assurance. Fifty-five years later he testified, "I have not experienced one doubt as to the genuineness of the experience."

Upon returning to his pastorate, he witnessed to the first ones he met that God had sanctified him wholly. They too had been seeking under his ministry and rejoiced that their young pastor had entered into this experience. Soon after, a large number of his best members entered into the experience of Christian perfection. His zeal and effective-ness led him from the circuit into full-time evangelism, and God blessed his ministry over the years.

65. Alfred Cookman (1828-71)

One of the shining lights in the holiness movement in the United States was Alfred Cookman. He and others like him gave a ring of authenticity to the doctrine they experienced and promoted.

Cookman, a Methodist minister, known as an ad-vocate of the doctrine of entire sanctification by faith, was noted equally, within and without his denomination, as an embodiment of that doctrine. Of him T. DeWitt Talmage said, "It was nothing so much I ever heard him say, or anything I every saw him do, that so impressed me as himself. He was the grace of the gospel impersonated . . . Sweep a circle of three feet around the cross of Jesus, and you take in all that there was of Alfred Cookman." One of his brethren said of him,

> Alfred Cookman was the best model of a Methodist preacher I ever knew. As a camp meeting preacher, [he] was a prince among his brethren. An announcement that he would preach always insured a large congregation. A sermon preached by him at the Camden Camp, upon the subject of entire sanctification, will never be forgotten by those who heard it. It was the clearest exposition of the great doctrine I ever heard. His appeals were irresistible, and swept all hearts. The fire which he kindled that day he drew from heaven.

As a boy preacher, Alfred Cookman prayed for the grace of entire sanctification. While pastor at New Town, Bishop Leonidas L. Hamline came to dedicate the new church and spent a week in special meetings, during which time the bishop spoke repeatedly and pointedly in private concerning the young pastor's religious experience. Together they prayed. Alfred made an entire consecration; henceforth he determined to "please God by believing that the altar (Spirit) sanctifieth the gift." Great peace came to his soul, followed by eight weeks of "light, strength, love, and blessing." Then at annual conference he grieved the Spirit, he confesses, by drifting into "foolish joking and story-telling." It was 10 years before he confessed, reconsecrated, and prayed through to a renewed Pentecostal experience. He remained in victory until in his own dying testimony, he went "sweeping through the gates, washed in the blood of the Lamb!" (See H. B. Ridgeway, *Life of Rev. Alfred Cookman* [London, 1875].)

66. Andrew Murray (1828-1917)

The name of Andrew Murray of South Africa is familiar wherever books on prayer and the devotional life are known. He is also among the honored greats of the modern holiness movement. Murray was born in Africa of a Scottish father and a Dutch mother. His father was a clergyman. Young Murray received his formal education in Europe and returned to South Africa as a clergyman in the Dutch Reformed church. While Andrew and his brother John were studying in Scotland, this area experienced a revival of religion in connection with the work of a young evangelist named William Burns. Deeply influenced by the moving of the Spirit of God in these meetings, both John and Andrew Murray felt led to the ministry. After seven years of study in Scotland, they continued three years in preparation for the ministry in Holland.

Holland experienced, around 1845, a revival of religion. A small group of praying people kept alive the revival in Amsterdam for a decade after 1845. At this time students at Utrecht formed a religious society whose purpose was to study the subjects required for ministers "in the spirit of the revival." This small and despised religious society were comparable to the "Holy Club" at Oxford, 100 years before, which led to the beginning of Methodism. John and Andrew Murray were participants in this small religious society.

After three years, following his conversion in Scotland under William Burns, Andrew Murray had matured considerably and had become convinced of his vocation as a clergyman.

Murray's first pastoral assignment was a large congregation at Bloemfontein. It was a vast parish mostly of Dutch settlers and farmers. He was a vigorous and energetic pastor, interested not only in his immediate flock, but full of missionary vision and zeal for areas on the frontier. His ministry included all classes from the prosperous to the destitute. His second pastorate at Worcester coincided with a great revival in this church, roughly simultaneous with the revival in the United States just prior to the outbreak of the Civil War.

During his second pastorate at Worcester, news reached his congregation of the 1858-60 revival movement in America. The leaders and laymen of his congregation longed for a similar moving of the Spirit in their midst. A veritable Pentecost occurred when a black girl about 15 years of age rose at the back of a hall and asked if she could suggest a hymn. Then she read the hymn verse and prayed in such moving tones that the leader of the meeting thought that he heard the sound of wind in the distance. The building itself seemed to be shaken and the whole congregation broke out in audible prayer. This occurred in the absence of the pastor, Andrew Murray, whose reaction to the phenomena was negative at first.

But soon after, in a meeting led by Pastor Murray, there was again a sound in the distance of a rushing mighty wind which resulted in the whole congregation breaking out spontaneously in prayer. A foreigner who had just come from America told the pastor that this was the Spirit of God moving exactly as was happening in America. Andrew Murray then became instrumental in promoting the revival, not only in his own parish but also in many other nearby parishes.

Murray experienced his own personal Pentecost and was a very effective speaker to congregations in many parts of the world. He spoke at Keswick in 1879, and an outpouring of the Spirit of God was experienced by that congregation. At the invitation of Dwight L. Moody, he addressed the Northfield Conference in Massachusetts. The burden of his message was the feeble life in the churches and the need for revival. Increasingly he came to present the necessity of going on to perfection after conversion. Referring to his own experience, he said,

> You have heard how I've pressed upon you the two stages in the Christian life and the step from one to the other. The first ten years of my spiritual life were on the lower stage; while I was zealous, earnest and happy in my work there was a burning in my heart, a dissatisfaction and restlessness. My justification was as clear as noonday, but I had no power for service. My mind became exercised about the baptism of the Holy Spirit. I gave myself to God as perfectly as I could to receive the baptism of the Holy Spirit.
>
> Now I have learned to place myself before God everyday as a vessel to be filled with His Spirit. With the deepest feeling of my soul, I can say that I am satisfied with Jesus now, yet when we are brought into the holiest of all we are only beginning to make a right position with the Father.

Increasingly Murray, under the influence of William Law, John Wesley, and others, became increasingly articulate and emphatic about the need of a second crisis experience in which the fullness of the blessing of God is added to the believer following his justification. In retrospect, Murray had many of the qualities that made William Law, John Wesley, and Alexander Whyte so effective as devotional and revivalistic leaders.

67. **J. A. Wood** (1828-1905)

J. A. Wood was a Methodist pastor in the early days of the holiness movement in America. He was author of the indispensable holiness classic *Perfect Love*, and writes thus of his entrance into the "more excellent way."

> After justification I was often convicted of remaining corruption of heart and of my need of purity. I desired to be a decided Christian and a useful member of the church; but was often conscious of deep-rooted

inward evils and tendencies in my heart unfriendly to godliness . . . They occupied a place in my heart which I knew should be possessed by the Holy Spirit. They were the greatest obstacles to my growth in grace, and rendered my service to God but partial.

I was often more strongly convicted of my need of inward purity than I ever had been of my need of pardon . . . I seldom studied the Bible without conviction of my fault in not coming up to the Scripture standard of salvation.

I often commenced seeking holiness, but at no time made any marked progress; for as I read and prayed, some duty was presented which I was unwilling to perform, and so I relapsed into indifference. . . .

Being so often convicted of my need of perfect love, and failing to obtain it, I, after a while, like many others, became somewhat skeptical in regard to the Wesleyan doctrine of entire sanctification, as a distinct work, subsequent to regeneration. I held no clear or definite ideas in regard to the blessing of perfect love, thought of it, and taught it, as only a deeper work of grace, or a little more religion. I taught, as many do now, a gradual growth into holiness, and threw the whole matter into indefiniteness and vague generalities.

. . . If a pious brother exhorted the preachers to seek sanctification, or the members to put away worldliness, tobacco, and gaudy attire, and seek holiness, I was distressed in spirit, and disposed to find fault.

Finally, he was convinced by some godly members of his church that he must confess his need publicly and seek this blessing. No sooner had he made this decision than

in an instant I felt a giving away in my heart, so sensible and powerful, that it appeared physical rather than spiritual; a moment after I felt an indescribable sweetness permeating my entire being . . . I was conscious that Jesus had me in his arms, and that the heaven of heavens was streaming through and through my soul in such beams of light and overwhelming love and glory, as can never be uttered. . . . He melted, cleansed and filled, and thrilled my feeble, unworthy soul with holy, sin-consuming power.

William McDonald also described Wood's experience on this occasion:

> About the first of September he took some eighty of his members to the Binghamton district camp meeting. Up to the last day of the meeting the subject of sanctification was constantly before his mind. He struggled hard and was in the deepest distress of mind, but said nothing to any one of his state. A faithful member of his church approached him and said; "Brother Wood, there is no use in trying to dodge this question. You know your duty. If you will lead the way and define your position as a seeker of entire sanctification, you will find that many of your members will do the same."
>
> After a few moments' reflection he resolved to go into his tent after preaching, and request his members to pray for him, that God would sanctify his soul. This to him was the supreme moment. The decision was made; and with the surrender came a clear and powerful assurance of victory, sweet as honey to his taste, and sensible as if some physical change had occurred.

Under the influence of the holy spell which rested upon him, he walked up into the stand to listen to the word of the Lord and just as the text was announced,

> "Let us hear the conclusion of the whole matter," the fulness of the divine baptism fell upon him, which completely prostrated him for nearly three hours. To him it was like the glory of heaven streaming through his soul, or as if he had marched through the gates of the city of God to the very bosom of Jesus. The work was done. (Wm. McDonald, *Advocate of Bible Holiness*, January, 1882, p. 19)

68. H. V. Degen (fl. 1851)

Perhaps the earliest nondenominational periodical of the modern holiness movement was the one founded by

"Father Merritt" entitled the *Guide to Holiness*. In 1851 Rev. H. V. Degen became its editor. Of his own personal Pentecost he writes:

> For nine years I labored in the itinerant ministry, holding up a standard to which I had not yet attained. This "reaching forth unto those things which are before," had a happy effect on both my ministry and personal experience. It was while stationed in this city (Boston), some forty years ago, that I received at the yearly Eastham gathering (camp meeting), on Cape Cod, a most remarkable spiritual baptism.
>
> In a manner and to a degree never before realized, Christ was presented to my mind as the source not only of justifying but of preserving grace; that he was able not only to save but to save to the uttermost—i.e., through all time (or, as the margin has it, evermore); that as the Captain of our salvation, he was not only the victor, but the insurer of victory to us; that he came not only to save but to keep—and that to make him available to us in this twofold relation, our faith must be a continuous childlike trust in his word and work.

One cannot read over the experiences of the leaders in the early days of the holiness movement without noting the remarkable freshness, sincerity, and variety of their testimonies. Few used stereotyped phrases, most were plain spoken, with a frank zeal for a great cause without narrow sectarian zeal. They did not exploit a great doctrine for a personal profit or prestige. Such is the impression one may get from these 19th-century witnesses.

69. James Hudson Taylor I (1832-1905)

There are "apostles; and some, prophets; and some, evangelists; and some, pastors and teachers" (Eph. 4:11). James H. Taylor is due the title of "apostle" because of the pioneering work forever linked with his name. He was founder of the China Inland Mission, which four decades after its founding numbered nearly 1,000 missionaries and over 1,000 mission stations throughout the interior of China. Some £1½ million (not dollars) had by that time been given *without solicitation*, simply in answer to believing prayer.

Taylor's parents were Methodists and deeply devout. From them young Hudson learned the disciplines of the Christian life at a tender age. On the centennial observance of the founding of Methodism (1839) this child began to show the love for Christ and for others that so characterized his adult life. Later he backslid but was brought back to the Lord alone while reading a tract at the very time his mother and sister were interceding for his salvation; henceforth it was "not I, but Christ whose finished work in the atonement brought peace and joy." He was then 17 years of age. Thereafter he rejoiced in the awareness of sonship and looked for opportunities for witness and service. This initial joy in the Lord was followed by periods of leanness, an awareness of indwelling sin, "painful deadness of soul and much conflict" often "disappointed in its struggles with sin."

At this time of spiritual crisis, instead of being content with the "lower path," he determined to "go on with the Lord, trusting His strength and faithfulness to pardon, loose and cleanse, to sanctify . . . wholly." At this period his attention was called to an article in *Wesleyan* magazine entitled "The Beauty of Holiness." This intensified his longing to find "victory over self and sin." To his sister Amelia he wrote on December 2, 1849, "Pray for me. I am seeking entire sanctification. Oh that the Lord would take away my heart of stone and give me a heart of flesh . . . my heart longs for this perfect holiness." That night in spiritual agony he was led to make a complete renunciation of the self-life and yielded himself fully "to God and God's service." In his own words:

113

> Never shall I forget the feeling that came over me then. Words can never describe it. I felt I was in the presence of God, entering into covenant with the Almighty. . . . Something seemed to say, "Your prayer is answered, your conditions are accepted." And from that time the conviction never left me that I was called to China.

To his sister Amelia he wrote, "He has cleansed me from all sin, from all my idols. He has given me a new heart. Glory, glory, glory to His ever blessed name!"

His biographer adds,

> From that day onward life was on another plane. The Lord had led him, satisfied his soul, and spoken again the meek, completing word, 'Follow Me.' Outwardly it was manifest that a great change had come over him. Inwardly there was a deep subjection to the will of God, resting upon a profound and unalterable sense of what that will was for him. And with this came new purity and power, a steady growth in grace, and fulness of blessing that carried him through all the testing and preparation of the next few years.

Such was the spiritual secret of the man of limited physical assets who was led to pioneer work in China which has made a deep and lasting influence not only in reaching thousands for Christ in Asia but setting an example of faith which has directly influenced the ideals and strategies of modern faith missions.

As a Catholic priest from Austria said to me recently in Wulai, Taiwan, "He was a very famous person." Read the full story in Dr. and Mrs. Howard Taylor's *Hudson Taylor in Early Years: The Growth of a Soul* (London: 1911).

70. **Hannah Whitall Smith** (1832-1911)

One of the classics in the library of Christian devotion is Mrs. Smith's book *The Christian's Secret of a Happy*

Life. Many, including Dr. E. Stanley Jones, have been led into the experience of full salvation due to the influence of this book. Her husband, Logan Pearsall Smith, was very effective in evangelistic work in the holiness movement in England. Mrs. Smith was welcomed as a very effective Bible expositor and later, after her husband's illness, gave herself more and more to writing. All of her books are characterized by a concern for holiness of heart and life and the note of joy in Christian service.

Hers was a Quaker background. This may explain the lack of certain theological specifics, which one encounters in other books of the kind by theologians, but there is no mistaking the scriptural validity and experiential authenticity of the Christian life she describes. In her discussion of the question of whether this doctrine is scriptural, she cites a series of passages in the New Testament giving evidence that the Christian is to expect deliverance from indwelling sin, that salvation is total and adequate, not partial. Typical of her trenchant style is this conjecture:

> Can we, for a moment, suppose that the Holy God, who hates sin in the sinner, is willing to tolerate it in the Christian, and that He has even arranged the plan of salvation in such a way as to make it impossible for those who are saved from the guilt of sin, to find deliverance from its power? (*The Christian's Secret of a Happy Life* [Westwood, N.J.: Fleming H. Revell Co., 1952], p. 21)

Mrs. Smith continues,

> Holy men of [t]his generation, . . . of our own, as well as of generations of long past, have united in declaring that the redemption accomplished for us by our Lord Jesus Christ on the cross at Calvary, is a redemption from the power of sin as well as from its guilt, and that He *is* able to save to the uttermost all who come unto God by Him (p. 22).

As a result of extensive acquaintance with people in

their spiritual need, Mrs. Smith dealt extensively with difficulties concerning faith and doubts and failures. She stressed God's side in making men holy and man's responsibility for availing himself of this grace. She described clearly "how to enter in." She correctly emphasizes that it is not an *attainment* but an *obtainment*. We can do nothing but *ask* for it and *receive* it, since it is God's gift through Christ. Of this she says no one would boast of having acquired a gift but would be grateful as a recipient.

Concerning the difficulty of just believing and obeying, she tells of a conversation with a physician in which she asks the doctor if he would accept as a patient a person who would refuse to give a full commitment to his treatment. The doctor replied he would only take the case upon the condition that his instructions would be obeyed implicitly. "This," Mrs. Smith said, "is the consecration that God requires."

She tells of a Christian who confided to another of his deep distress at his efforts to find deliverance from indwelling sin and victory in Christ and who concluded by saying, "All these efforts have been in vain; there is nothing left to do but to trust the Lord." To this his friend replied with sympathy, "Alas, has it come to that?" as if this were the riskiest thing of all! Thus in nontheological but scriptural phraseology, a conviction reinforced by Christian experience, Mrs. Smith not only testified to her own generation but to many generations since. Hers is a legacy which will endure.

71. **W. B. Godbey** (1833-1920)

Evangelist Godbey was a remarkable evangelist and teacher. He was born near Somerset, Ky., in 1833. Here he lived on a farm until the age of 20, helping his preacher-father clear the brush. Godbey was known to his admirers as much for his eccentricities as for his effectiveness in winning souls. He speaks of his conversion at the age of 3, but for want of further training remained in a backslidden state for years. He was a chronic seeker, constantly under conviction.

At the age of 16, however, in November, 1849, he attended a Baptist revival. Here he fell under deep conviction and sought God at the altar but failed to find victory. By eleven o'clock a friend took him to his home lest conviction leave him and he revert to his backslidden state. Young Godbey did not sleep but spent the night in spiritual distress. The next day at the church he found the place crowded, with jesting and profanity going on outside, which so distressed him that he went to the woods. There he finally came to the end of himself, abandoned his own self-esteem, and completely yielded himself to God. He reports, "That mountain burden rolled away and I found myself leaping for joy." Until the end of his life this wooded site remained a hallowed place in his life.

He had no teaching upon a further work of grace or entire sanctification and so did not seek. Although his conversion was witnessed by the Holy Spirit, it was not long until he felt a further need which he could not identify or explain. After talking with some Christians, he was advised that the best he could expect in the Christian life was conflict until death. Meanwhile, he continued teaching school, educating himself quite largely, and worked his way through the Baptist college in Georgetown, Ky. During these years he was very effective in winning souls and personally growing in grace, but he had heard nothing about sanctification. What he read in Wesley's works he attributed to Wesley's misunderstanding.

It was not until 19 years after his conversion that he met an old woman, illiterate, who claimed the experience of perfect love. She could not read the Bible or explain her experience scripturally, yet "the testimony of old sister Baxter . . . was so clear and her testimony so positive, collaborated by an unearthly radiance lingering in her face and flashing from her eyes, that it had an effect to convict me." Some time later he preached at a protracted meeting. There was a good response; and while several were seeking at the altar of prayer, a very old woman grasped the pastor's arm and, speaking more loudly than she intended, said, "O Brother Donaldson, please do not put up that little fop anymore lest you ruin our revival."

Godbey heard it and said, "It was to me a thunderbolt from a cloudless sky." This characterization by the old saint broke his heart and he never survived it. He said, "The Holy Spirit used these two mothers of Israel to culminate the conviction that had been lingering in my heart for nineteen years" (*Autobiography*, p. 93). He spent hours that afternoon in the woods crying to God to satisfy the longing of his heart and give him the glorious liberty which he had been seeking for 19 years since his conversion. When God met his need that night, he described it as like the inundation of a mighty sea: "I have been basking in that ocean ever since. O, the incommunicable sweetness of perfect love" (p. 94).

As he told people of this wonderful experience, they assured him it was a second conversion. However, he later met a Methodist theologian who, after hearing Godbey's report of this experience, said, "Godbey, if you had not been converted none of us have . . . it is that old Methodist experience of sanctification or Christian perfection by which by the grace of God you have entered" (p. 95). He said that this was the work of grace called Christian perfection which he heard when he was a boy.

Godbey then went on to read books by Wesley and Fletcher on the Bible and Christian perfection. "With a new and glorious sunburst they spangled the inspired pages." Later he said, "I have seen regeneration and sanctification standing out as conspicuously distinct as the Alleghenys and the Rockies with the great Mississippi valley rolling between. Sanctification is the most remarkable epoch in my experience marking a radical revolution in my life" (p. 96). After teaching school and occasionally preaching, he became a full-time conference preacher and evangelist. This occurred in 1868, "fifteen years before the holiness movement crossed the Ohio River" (p. 100). Thereafter he emphasized the experience of entire sanctification, not without conflict, but he preached with far greater effectiveness than he had before.

72. **Adoniram Judson Gordon** (1836-95)

To those interested in missions, one of the great, familiar names of the 19th century is that of a clergyman who for 25 years served as pastor of the Clarendon Street Baptist Church in Boston. Born in a strict Calvinistic home in New England, he was thoroughly committed to the Calvinism of his parents, to a high view of Scripture, and to a personal commitment to the Lordship of Jesus Christ. His parents named him in honor of the great Baptist missionary pioneer to Burma, Adoniram Judson.

Following a very effective pastorate, A. J. Gordon was summoned to Northfield, Mass., to share with Dwight L. Moody in the summer conference there. At this time Northfield was a great evangelical center. Famous visitors included James Hudson Taylor, Alexander Duff, Henry Drummond, A. T. Pierson, Andrew Murray, Andrew Bonar, F. B. Meyer, and other evangelical leaders.

On one occasion Dwight L. Moody, at the request of the students, had given his own experience of the baptism of the Spirit. After 10 days of preaching and praying, Gordon was found with others at the midnight hour praying for the infilling of the Holy Spirit. A companion described his seeking in these words: "The holy man poured out his soul with a freedom and unction indescribable." This source adds, "I have no doubt that he received then a divine touch which enobled his personal life and made his ministry of ever increasing spirituality and of ever widening breadth of sympathy" (Earnest B. Gordon, *Adoniram Judson Gordon* [Revell, 1896], p. 178).

Soon after this, Gordon was at a seaside resort leading men to Christ. The result of the Spirit's infilling at this midnight hour was obvious as he worked with people seeking the Lord. A friend noted, "He seemed filled with the Spirit, he could not talk about commonplace matters. He said he had had 'a great blessing.'"

Towards the end of his ministry, Gordon stressed more and more the importance of the Spirit-filled life. This concern he expressed in a book entitled *The Twofold Life*. His lectures often were on the subject of "The Ministry of the Spirit" and "The Holy Spirit in Missions." Increasingly he was "experiencing personally the presence of the Spirit as he climbed steadily to the table lands of a higher life."

Gordon thought of the work of the Spirit as threefold: sealing, filling, and anointing. Sealing is the assurance of salvation; the filling is the enduement of power; the anointing, as John's Epistle indicates, is knowledge. In Gordon's own words,

> It costs much to attain this power. It costs self-surrender and humiliation and the yielding up of our most precious things to God . . . but when we are really in that power, we shall feel this difference: that, whereas before it was hard for us to do the easiest things, now it is easy for us to do the hardest. (p. 365)

Thus A. J. Gordon joined the witnesses, including others in the Reformed tradition, who experienced the importance of being "endued with power from on high."

73. Dwight L. Moody (1837-99)

If one were to choose a list of the 10 most effective evangelists in Christian history, the name of Dwight Lyman Moody would surely be among the 10. At this distance it is difficult to fully grasp the dimensions of that dedicated life. We see him with limited formal education but a vigorous and dynamic personality wholly absorbed in his work.

He was born on February 5, 1837, at Northfield, Mass., a lovely rural town in the western part of the state near the Berkshire Mountains. He did not like his schoolwork, nor did he like farm work. He was really a "dropout" of both when, at the age of 17, he went to Boston to work in his uncle's shoe store. Here his uncle accepted him and gave him employment under the condition that he would attend the Mount Vernon Congregational Church regularly, avoid questionable places and amusements, and keep off the streets at night.

His Sunday School teacher was Mr. Edward Kimball. Moody had been attending the class for a year before the teacher became concerned for his soul. On April 21, 1855, Kimball determined to go to the store to speak to Dwight about his spiritual condition. He found the young man at the back of the store wrapping up shoes. He placed a hand on his shoulder and made what he considered "a weak appeal about Christ and His love."

But this was enough to reach Moody's heart. In Moody's own words, "I went out of doors and I fell in love with the bright sun shining over the earth. I never loved the sun before. And when I heard the birds singing their sweet song in the Boston Common, I fell in love with the birds. I was in love with all creation." Moody had been born again. But it was a year before the church, after considerable misgivings, accepted him into full membership.

Soon after, Moody left for Chicago. What if Mr. Kimball had not followed the Spirit's prompting to speak to Moody about his spiritual condition?

Throughout the rest of Moody's ministry he believed that others like himself could find instantaneous deliverance from the guilt of sin through the grace of Christ. Moody was constantly seeking souls in addition to his secular employment. After service in the Civil War, he returned to his Sunday School work in Chicago as a lay pastor. Gradually through overwork and a sense of spiritual and mental inadequacy he sensed (by 1866) that something was wrong. He spent the spring of 1867 in England seeking to get inspiration from the spiritual leaders in that country. He was especially impressed by Spurgeon's sermons. He was a better man under the influence of Spurgeon, but he still felt inadequate. Later he studied faith under George Muller. Harry Morehouse urged upon him the importance of biblical preaching. This helped, but was not enough. Even attending the general assembly in Edinburgh before returning did him "a world of good"; however, all these things left him with a feeling of inadequacy.

In 1869, Moody noticed two elderly Free Methodist women in his noon prayer meetings. They were Mrs. Cook and Mrs. Snow. In the words of R. L. Day, "He knew that he was deficient somewhere; and he knew they knew it, too." As Mr. Moody later told his friend F. B. Meyer, "The ladies said, 'You are good; but there is something you have not got; we are praying that it may come.'" They were praying that he might be filled with the Spirit. This annoyed Moody considerably. He already had the largest congregation in Chicago and was winning more people to Christ than anyone else in that area. As Day puts it, "He was belligerent toward those dreadful women when they were present; and miserably lonely when they didn't come" (*Bush Aglow*, p. 124).

If Moody had died then in his 34th year, no one would ever have written his biography, nor would any institutions have been named after him. He remembered his friend Morehouse saying that he needed to study more and that he should study one book of the Bible. After another service, one of the elderly sisters who had been praying for him said quietly, "Lad, Jehovah is dealing with thee." As Day puts it,

> These mothers of Israel were all love and gentleness. They knew he was sincere, they knew he was unselfish, and they loved him for it, but that wasn't enough. They prayed for him. He was humbled to the dust. After they left, he came back into the parlor and covered his face with his hands.

Later, as reported by F. B. Meyer,

> . . . one afternoon in New York, he was walking along when an irresistible impulse came upon him to be alone. He looked around. Where could he go? What was to be done? He remembered a friend living not far away so he rushed to his house and demanded a room where he could be alone. There he remained several hours and there he received the baptism of the Holy Ghost. When he returned to Chicago and began to speak, the Godly woman who had spoken to him before time said, "You have it now." And the wonderful power which Moody exercised over his fellowmen he owed to that touch of fire. It never left him. People were attracted. What happened when he visited England, happened wherever he went.

Later, as he recalled it, he cried to God, "Deliver me from myself. Take absolute sway. Give Thy Holy Spirit." Previously he had been trying to pump water out of a well that seemed dry, then God made his soul like an artesian well that could never fail of water. After that in Chicago, in a new building which followed the fire on December 24,

1871, before a vast crowd, he saw the two ladies that had been praying for him. Now he *rejoiced* to see them in the audience!

74. **Amanda Berry Smith** (1837-1915)

Born in slavery, converted in a revival meeting, married at the age of 17, reclaimed afterwards, this black woman later became an international evangelist. Her witness to full salvation took her all over America, then to England, India, and Africa. How was this possible?

While bending over the washtub, weeping over family troubles, a friend told her, "When you get sanctified, you will have enduring grace." Thereafter she often prayed, "O Lord, sanctify my soul and give me enduring grace." She found that baptism by immersion and washing the saints' feet did not help.

But she heard John Inskip preach at a camp meeting service on the text, "Put on the new man, which after God is created in righteousness and true holiness" (Eph. 4:24). In simple faith she trusted God to do this for her. As she described it, "I seemed to go two ways at once—up and down. Such a wave came over me, and such a welling up of my heart. Oh, what glory filled my soul! The great vacuum in my soul began to fill up. I wanted to shout: 'Glory to Jesus,' but Satan said, 'Now if you make a noise, they will put you out.'" She almost quenched the Spirit as wave after wave swept through her soul as the sermon continued. Finally, during the singing of the last hymn, she could remain silent no longer. She shouted, "Glory to Jesus!" The power of the Lord came mightily upon her, prostrating her under its weight.

> The simplicity of her faith thereafter was wonderful . . . She learned to walk in the Spirit. Her flaming testimony was blest to many. Calls to camp and re-

vival services multiplied. The humble, earnest colored woman was owned of God in prayer, song, and testimony.

She is remembered as one of the brightest gems in the annals of the holiness movement.

75. **Phineas F. Bresee** (1838-1915)

Phineas Franklin Bresee served as a pastor in the Methodist church for over three decades in Iowa and later in California. He is known at Peniel Mission in Los Angeles, at Pasadena College in Pasadena, and as founder of the Church of the Nazarene. He was an ardent advocate of the Spirit-filled life and was very effective as preacher and pastor.

His religious depression began while he was serving as presiding elder and became serious while he pastored at Chariton. He described this experience to E. A. Girvin.

I had a big load of carnality on hand always, but it had taken the form of anger, and pride, and worldly ambition. At last, however, it took the form of doubt. It seemed as though I doubted everything. I thought it was intellectual, and undertook to answer it. I thought that probably I had gone into the ministry so early in life, that I had never answered the great questions of being, and of God, and of destiny and of sin and the atonement, and I undertook to answer these great questions. I studied hard to so answer them as to settle the problems that filled my mind with doubt.

Over and over again, I suppose a thousand times, I built and rebuilt the system of faith, and laid the foundation of revelation, the atonement, the new birth, destiny, and all that, and tried to assure myself of their truth. I would build a pyramid, and walk around about it and say, "It is so, I know it is so. It is in accord with revelation. It is in accord with my intuitions. It is in accord with history and human experience. It is so, and I do not question it." And I would not get through the assertions of my certainty, before the devil or something else, would say, "Suppose it isn't so, after all?" And my doubts would not be any nearer settled than they were before.

During the winter's protracted meeting at Chariton, Bresee came to the end of his doubt. In his own words he described this experience. "There came one of those awful, snowy, windy nights, such as blew across the Western plains occasionally, with the thermometer twenty degrees below zero. Not many were out to church that night. I tried hard to preach a little, the best I could. I tried to rally the people to the altar, the few that were there, and went back to the stove, and tried to get somebody to the Lord. I did not find anyone. I turned toward the altar; in some way it seemed to me that this was my time, and I threw myself down across the altar and began to pray for myself.

I had come to the point where I seemingly could not go on. My religion did not meet my needs. It seemed as though I could not continue to preach with this awful question of doubt on me, and I prayed and cried to the Lord. I was ignorant of my own condition. I did not understand in reference to carnality. I did not understand in reference to the provisions of the atonement.

I neither knew what was the matter with me, nor what would help me, and, as I cried to Him that night, He seemed to open heaven on me, and gave me, as I believe, the baptism with the Holy Ghost, though I did not know either what I needed, or what I prayed for. But it not only took away my tendencies to worldliness, anger and pride, but it also removed my doubt. For the first time, I apprehended that the conditions of doubt were moral instead of intellectual, and that doubt was a part of carnality that could only be removed as the other works of the flesh are removed.

H. D. Brown describes this experience after discussing it with Bresee.

After repeated conversation with Dr. Bresee concerning the events of the evening . . . there is a vivid picture in my mind of what occurred. It was a furious night. The storm of wind and snow raged without, while Dr. Bresee preached as best he could. Satan and the carnal mind poured upon him such a storm of doubt as equaled the raging elements without. Later in the service he went to the back of the room inviting sinners to come, but one by one they slipped away home and only a few of the Lord's earnest people lingered about the altar. In the midst of his sorrow he turned toward the altar and flung himself down crying, 'Now, Lord, what have you for me?' He unburdened his soul. He cried unto God for some sure foundation upon which his storm-tossed spirit might securely rest.

It is well to note that while the experience described did meet the deep need of Bresee, he did not have the theological understanding to comprehend its meaning for himself nor to describe it to his congregation in his preaching ministry. He himself said in later years of this experience, "Nobody got sanctified but myself, and I did not know anything about it." Although he could not define the experience in theological terms, there came into his personal life a deeper spirituality and greater confidence in his preaching, for he was no longer troubled with the assailing doubts and the evidences of pride. It was after his removal to California and his subsequent acquaintance with Drs. MacDonald and Watson that he learned the theology of his experience and went through the unusual mystical experience there that intensified his effectiveness as a holiness preacher. (See Donald P. Brickley, *Man of the Morning* [Kansas City: Nazarene Publishing House, 1960].)

76. John Pike (1840-1932)

Assurance is the key word in the report of this witness. Rev. John Pike, in 1882, thus related how he was "fully saved."

The Bible became my constant study, and it seemed as if the demands for holiness, the prayers for holiness, and the promises of holiness shone forth on every page . . . My soul became the furnace of such intense desire, that everything else seemed to shrink into insignificance in comparison with this. I sank very low in my own estimation. I needed no argument to prove the presence of indwelling sin; I knew it by bitter experience. My convictions for innate depravity were deeper far than I ever experienced previous to my conversion. But the consciousness of God's favor was mine, and I knew it. . . .

I was satisfied that the consecration was now made complete, and I was authorized to believe that I was all the Lord's . . . My feelings of anxiety gave place to calm reliance upon the promise, "ye shall have it." I felt that something was coming, and I said:

"Come as thou wilt—I that resign;
But, oh my Saviour, come."

And he did come—glory be to his name forever! I was sitting at my study table, writing a business letter, when I felt an indescribable, sweet, hallowed feeling pervading my entire being, and with it came the assurance, double assured, that the Comforter had complete possession, and "I was every whit whole." The words seemed to run off my pen upon the paper, and in the midst of business matters I wrote:

"I have entered the valley of blessing so sweet,
And Jesus abides with me there!"

(*Advocate of Bible Holiness*, Feb., 1882)

77. Jane Cooper (fl. 1872)

The note of sincerity and authenticity is reflected in the words of this otherwise unknown witness of the way. In the *Arminian* magazine for August, 1872, the "Christian Experience of Jane Cooper" was published for the edification of its readers. She wrote:

My prayer has been, for these fourteen years past, that I may be nothing. And I praise God, I have reason to hope, that I come a little nearer to that blessed mark. I well know there is no happiness like that which flows from a constant sense that I am nothing, and Jesus is all! . . . I am contemptible in my own eyes; yet I feel I am precious in his sight, who has paid so dear a price for me. My soul is broken before the Lord, and desires to follow him as the shadow follows the substance. He has my heart, and reigns the Lord of all my wishes and desires. I rejoice ever more in a constant union and oneness of spirit with the Lord Jesus: and pray without ceasing as the desire of my soul is going out to him at all times and in all places.

The paradox of self-realization through self-abnegation is well illustrated in this testimony. We seldom hear, in young and robust America, about desiring to be nothing, and it is wholesome to all but morbid souls to remember that Paul said, "Ye are dead, and your life is hid with Christ in God. When Christ, who is our life, shall appear, then shall ye also appear with him in glory" (Col. 3:3-4). The path to self-realization is self-renunciation.

78. **C. G. Moore** (fl. 1874)

Methodism began at Oxford University among the Holy Club, including John and Charles Wesley and George Whitefield. In a similar manner, the holiness movement known as the Keswick Convention also began at Oxford in 1874. The spiritual blessing which this meeting gave to an English clergyman, Rev. C. G. Moore, is typical of how thousands of others were blessed in a similar manner. Mr. Moore reports having attended at Oxford in 1874 the "union meeting for the promotion of scriptural holiness." This man's father had been influenced by Charles G. Finney. As a result of Finney's work, he states:

What great and searching conviction I passed through. How relentlessly the whole theme of Christ was pressed upon my conscience. Through these experiences, terrible at the time, I am sure I owe some of the most precious elements of my spiritual life. It was my joy to spend myself in Christ's service, and his blessing was not withheld from my ministry; but how much was lacking!

Pastor Moore attended the Oxford Conference with this acknowledgment of personal need. At this conference he had an interview with Mr. Pearsall Smith, husband of Hannah Whitall Smith, and, as a result of the interview with him, and upon reading his wife's book, he went to the Oxford meeting where he found three things that were especially helpful: *(a)* a clearer understanding of the New Testament emphasis upon faith; *(b)* "a new spirit and atmosphere for Christian life. I had never been in meetings where the Holy Spirit had such power and liberty, and where his choice fruits of love, joy, peace, meekness, and gentleness were so plentiful"; *(c)* a vision of Christ "enclosed, interested, loving, [and in] helpful contact with the whole life of his disciples." Pastor Moore continued by saying,

> I returned home from Oxford somewhat dazed by the new glory that had burst upon my view, but exceeding joyful, and duly purposed in God's strength to persevere in my poor attempts to live my life by the faith of the Son of God. From that hour to this he has been my faithful, ever-present Lord, Savior, and friend. Of course, I began to pass on to my people the good things I had learned, and the fruits of that ministry abide to this day.

This testimony is typical of the many which attended this Oxford Conference and which led in turn to a similar conference at Keswick in the Cambridge area of England which continues to this day and has been duplicated in many parts of the world. Thus the modern holiness movement of today is in three main branches. The main branch is the Methodist tradition stressing not only the filling of the Spirit but also the cleansing from indwelling sin. The Keswick Convention influence also stresses the Spirit-filled life and the cleansing from sin but comes short of saying that we have been delivered from all sin, thus stressing the process rather than the crisis, or rather crisis leading to process. Third, the modern Pentecostal movement which stresses the cleansing and being filled with the Spirit, but adds speaking in an unknown tongue. Probably the scriptural truth lies between the crisis stressed among the Wesleyans and the process stressed in the Keswick Convention. Scriptural stress is on both the process and the crisis.

79. **Canon Harford-Battersby** (fl. 1875)

The Keswick Convention was a result of Canon Harford-Battersby from the parish at Keswick, England, who passed through "a remarkable spiritual change at the Oxford Conference of 1874." He returned eager that his parishioners "should share with him the blessing which had transformed his life, and which, he was convinced, would have the same influence on all who would receive it." The following year this pastor with one of his laymen opened "a convention for the promotion of practical holiness." It convened at Keswick and was held in a tent holding about 600 people. From this humble beginning the movement has spread worldwide and has been a blessing to untold thousands. Like camp meetings in North America, the Keswick Conventions are designed primarily for the deepening of the spiritual life of the believers. The conventions consist of Bible study, of prayer, of testimonies, and of preaching. Usually after the evening preaching service, an after-meeting is held in which people are urged to seek personal cleansing and filling with the Spirit. Those who attend the convention are committed

Christians including many Christian workers who "come to Keswick cast down, restless, selfish, powerless, . . . and they have gone away with lives transformed." The theme of the conventions is to forsake the first principles of Christ and "to press on to perfection." Victory is sought, not as a lifelong struggle after an impossible ideal, "but by the surrender of the individual to God, and the indwelling of the Holy Spirit."

One testimony from a man who had been transformed at the Keswick Convention follows:

> I felt it most difficult to stand, but in the way that God had spoken to me it was difficult not to stand. The common peace of God filled me, and I returned home at his absolute disposal. What of the nine years since? They have been on an absolutely different plane, both as to Christian work, and as to the presence of Christ; there has been indeed failure on my part, but every failure can now be seen to be one's own fault, and that which need not have been.

Another minister from Scotland told his experience of a second work of divine grace. He described how God had given him a revelation of himself and of his inward sins. He continued:

> Then he took my selflife, put it on the cross, and took me to be altogether his; he emptied my house and shattered my health, but through it all I never had such peace. Three years ago I came here and sat back of the platform in calm joy, having known the crushing and searching before I ever came to Keswick, the cleansing and the filling too, before I heard them spoken of here. You ask, does it last? I answer, he lasts. You ask, have you obtained holiness? I have no attainments, I have only an attitude, I am surrendered on my side, that is all: and my prayer is . . . "What thou canst not consume, cleanse; what thou canst not cleanse, consume; and what thou canst neither consume nor cleanse, that counteract by thine own presence."

These are two witnesses who were very effective as Christians and yet felt an inward lack but were led "into a most definite blessing and transformation with lasting effects."

80. Handley C. G. Moule (1841-1920)

Bishop Handley Carr Glyn Moule is known to Bible scholars as a commentator of unusual skill. It is reassuring to find men of diverse theological traditions being led by the Spirit of God to the "more excellent way" of perfect love. Bishop Moule was a man of deep humility and tender piety but would have nothing to do with "perfectionism" until he heard an address which convinced him that it was entirely scriptural that Christians should be completely victorious over sin. He sought and found the way of complete victory over self and sin, through Christ. He wrote:

> I dare to say that it is possible for those who really are willing to reckon on the power of the Lord, for keeping and victory, to lead a life in which his promises are taken as they stand, and are found to be true. It is possible to cast all our care on him daily, and to enjoy deep peace in doing it. It is possible to have the thoughts and imaginations of our hearts purified in the deepest meaning of the word, through faith. . . . It is possible, in the inner life of desire and feeling, to lay aside all bitterness, and wrath, and anger, and evil-speaking, every day and every hour. It is possible, . . . , to find that the things which formerly upset all our resolves to be patient, or pure, or humble, furnish today an opportunity—through him who loved us . . . to make sin powerless.
>
> These things are Divine possibilities, and because they are his work, the true experience of them will always cause us to bow lower at his feet, and to learn to thirst and long for more. We cannot possibly be satisfied with anything less than—each day, each hour,

each moment, in Christ, through the power of the Holy Spirit—to walk with God.

The emphasis that sets the Keswick Convention apart from other religious gatherings, and which also brought upon itself a large amount of condemnation from the old-line churches, was the expectation of victory over sin and failure. The *diagnosis* of pardon in Christ accompanied by a series of defeats was the same, but the Keswick *remedy* was different. The foremost theologian of Keswick was Bishop Moule, who stated, "It does not depend upon a wearisome struggle but on God's power to take the consecrated soul and to keep him." For

> the open secret of inward victory, for liberty and life and service through the trusted power of the indwelling Christ, Christ in us for our deliverance from sin, for our emancipation and maturity of self, for the conquest of temptation the entrance is a twin door called surrender and faith.

As Bishop Moule continued to affirm the Keswick message, he stated:

> Would we know the Christ in us in his power? We must yield ourselves to the Christ over us in his will, his rights. This great truth of Christ over us by every claim of lordship, sovereignty, and position is the other side of Keswick's distinctive message.

Influenced by Aristotle's definition of a slave as "a chattel that lives," Moule recognized himself henceforth as Christ's slave. Christ, he said, is

> my master, my possessor: absolute, not constitutional, supremely entitled to order me about all day. How delightful a thought that hands or head or voice are indeed the implements of the faithful slave kept at work for such an owner—his property and glad indeed to be sold. (Pollock, *The Keswick Story*, p. 75)

At Keswick visitors had their hunger intensified, their expectations raised, and were encouraged to expect deliverance now; but, the leaders hastened to add, the crisis of victory should be followed by process in maturity. Full surrender was seen as a beginning, not an end. Sanctification, not being complete in an instant, should involve progress cultivated by prayer. The study of the Scriptures, worship and service combined, balance the two thoughts of cleansing and consecration, deliverance and dedication. Before Bishop Moule died and 31 years after his second crisis experience, the learned bishop said, "God knows how imperfectly I've used my secret. I repent before him in great humiliation. But I know the secret, his open secret of victory and rest. And I know how different life has been for that secret."

81. A. B. Simpson (1843-1919)

Albert Benjamin Simpson, the son of a hard-working father and a godly mother, was born of Scottish ancestry on a farm in Prince Edward Island in Canada. He attended the Presbyterian church and grew up in a good, strict home. For 10 months as a youth he had sought God in anguish before finding saving faith in Jesus as Savior. After an intense spiritual struggle he experienced regeneration after reading about saving faith in Marshall, *The Gospel Mystery of Sanctification.* He attended Knox College in Toronto and was soon recognized as a student of exceptional promise and a gifted speaker. At 21 he was ordained and called as pastor of Knox Presbyterian Church, Hamilton, Ontario, a church famed for its distinguished pastors.

At his second church in Louisville, Ky., he preached revival, built a tabernacle, and was effective as a pastor and a pulpiteer. A great spiritual crisis occurred after he had been an effective gospel preacher and evangelistic pastor there for 10 years.

It was during the Whittle and Bliss revival that he sensed his lack of the power of the Spirit in his life. He had preached powerfully on justification as seen in Romans 5. But he knew little of sanctification as defined in Romans 6 and 8. Instead he experienced the frustration described in Romans 7. Fifteen years after his conversion, in his own words, "I got into another deep experience of conviction and I got out of that by believing in Jesus as my sanctifier" (A. E. Thompson, *A. B. Simpson, His Life and Work* [1960], p. 64). He afterwards recalled this second crisis in his spiritual development. "I look back with unutterable gratitude to that lonely and sorrowful night when . . . my heart's first full consecration was made, and with unreserved surrender I could say,

> 'Jesus, I my cross have taken
> All to leave and follow Thee.'"

He became convinced later that many refuse the Spirit's leading at this point and fail to enter into the fullness of faith.

He commented further after a study of Psalm 110:

> Consecration must come first and then sanctification. We can consecrate ourselves as freewill offerings; then God sanctifies us and clothes us with the beauties of his holiness. The consecration is ours; the sanctification is His. (p. 66)

Elsewhere he expressed the change in these words:

> The indwelling of the Holy Ghost in the human spirit is quite distinct from the work of regeneration. In Ezekiel 36:26 they are most clearly distinguished. The one is described as taking away of "the stony heart" and giving "a heart of flesh"; of the other it is said, "I will put my Spirit within you . . . !" (p. 67)

He added:

> There is a great difference between our receiving power from the Holy Ghost and our receiving the Holy

Ghost as our power. In the latter case . . . it is the Person who dwells within us who possesses and exercises all the gifts and power of our ministry, and only as we abide in Him.

He warned that it "is not sanctification as a state, but Christ as a living person." At first he sought the experience, later he sought the Lord; first the gift, but later the Giver.

In *Wholly Sanctified*, Simpson wrote, "The true attitude of the consecrated is that of a constant yielding and constant receiving. This last view of sanctification gives boundless scope to our spiritual progress."

The significance of A. B. Simpson's life is that with his Presbyterian background, the leading into the Spirit-filled life of holiness was the result of God's direct dealing.

He was led to stress the moment-by-moment dependence on the Lord, but the Giver more than the gift.

With his concern with sanctity and power was the concern for the unreached both in the evangelistic outreach at home and missionary outreach abroad. The result was the Christian and Missionary Alliance, whose worldwide influence is so beneficial.

82. **Beverly Carradine** (b. 1848)

Dr. Beverly Carradine was one of the great leaders in the modern holiness movement. As a Methodist preacher, he states that he always believed in the doctrine of holiness as the teaching of his church; at his ordination he had hesitatingly affirmed his expectation of being made perfect in love in this life, but the experience was only dimly glimpsed "afar off." He writes:

My conversion was bright and thorough. No one doubted my spirituality in the ministry. For twelve years or more preceding my sanctification I never put my head on my pillow at night without first obtaining a sense of my acceptance with God. My first vivid impression of sin in my heart was through a sudden loss of temper, months after my conversion.

. . . The thing that startled me was that when the temper burst forth it came out full-grown. A year later the same thing occurred. For years after that it flamed out again in a protracted meeting where I became vexed with the stubbornness of the unconverted. On a fly leaf in my Bible I wrote down a number of dark things that I found in my heart, and which I felt ought not to be there. One was levity, another uncharitable speech, and still another an unsanctified ambition . . . As the years rolled by I added to the dark list on the fly leaf of my Bible until I counted sixteen specifications in the bill of charges, which, under the light of the Spirit, I had made out against myself.

. . . I became convicted under my own preaching of the need of a deeper cleansing than I had ever before received, and an enduement of power along with it . . . Nearly nine months after this, . . . my soul was bitterly wrenched in an unutterable agony to be rid of a dark indwelling of something that made itself felt as I prayed. . . . The dark something had been taken out of my heart, and . . . the writer knows that for six years he has had perfect inward deliverance and rest.

After 13 years in a regenerated experience he publicly sought the baptism of the Holy Spirit at a camp meeting after preaching the sermon. He wanted

not so much a power to keep from all sin, but a deadness to sin. I wanted to be able to turn upon sin and the world the eye and ear and heart of a dead man. I wanted perfect love to God and man, and a perfect rest in my soul all the time. This dark "something" that prevented this life I laid on the altar, and asked God to consume it as by fire. I never asked God once at this time for pardon. That I had in my soul already. But it was cleansing, sin eradication I craved. My prayer was for sanctification.

After a battle of consecration came a battle of faith.

For three days he lived in a constant state of faith and prayer. The witness came on the morning of the third day.

> By some delicate instinct or intuition of soul I recognized the approach and descent of the Holy Ghost. My faith arose to meet the blessing. In another minute I was literally prostrated by the power of God. I recognized it all the while as the baptism of fire. I felt I was being consumed. I knew it was sanctification . . . as though the name was written across the face of the blessing and upon every wave of glory that rolled in upon my soul. (*Sanctification*, pp. 10-21)

The sequence: confession, consecration, faith, assurance, victorious living!

Twentieth-Century Witnesses

83. George Fox DeVol (1871-1917)

The family named DeVol, devout members of the Society of Friends, has cast a long shadow on Christian missions in China. Born on a farm near Glens Falls, N.Y., a graduate of Earlham College and New York University (M.D.), George was a devout lad from his childhood. As a child he found Christ as Savior after a period of conviction for sin. He wrote, afterward, "I can never forget the glad, sweet morning, following the evening I was converted, as I awoke to find myself a new child. All the world seemed brighter . . . I was born again and given a new heart."

While he was at Earlham College, Dr. J. Campbell White visited the campus in behalf of the Student Volunteer Movement. Young George signed the pledge: "God permitting, it is my purpose to become a foreign missionary."

Years later, as a medical missionary in China, Dr. George DeVol became increasingly aware that he must present himself a "living sacrifice." "He was certain that he needed, and must have, the purifying experience of entire sanctification."

> The way was plain, so plain that he took the step of faith and obtained "the promise of the Father!" Henceforth with undivided heart he was to be a love-slave of Christ. He had entered into the rest promised to the people of God, and peace filled his soul. He had been a devout Christian; now he was a radiant one.

Although an efficient and busy surgeon, his concern for the soul was equally his concern. At the summer retreat for missionaries at Kuling, China, he conducted a well-attended devotional service. The emphasis was upon "the sanctifying work of the Holy Spirit. Through this ministry, many were led into the experience of entire sanctification." The result was a formation of "The Chain of Wit-

143

ness" to heart purity, the purpose of which was to increase the number of such witnesses until "the experience of heart cleansing might encircle the globe." Along with his medical practice he was often called to address conferences, and he continued to witness to the Spirit-filled life until the triumphant home-going at Luho, site of the Friends Mission work in China.

84. **John Wesley Hughes** (1852-1932)

John Wesley Hughes was a Methodist pastor in Kentucky for 12 years and later an effective evangelist before becoming founder and president of Asbury College (in 1890).

During 13 years as a preacher he hungered for "a deeper work of grace." Under the preaching of W. B. Godbey he was convinced that it was not enough to be an effective child of God, but that he needed a cleansing and renewal at a deeper level of existence. At an altar service while praying with seekers, the Holy Spirit impressed him with his own spiritual need. Soon he was overpowered by the Spirit and lost consciousness. His first words upon recovering consciousness were, "Lord, it is enough. I can bear no more." The evangelist announced, "Brother Hughes is sanctified."

In a revival soon afterward God mightily used him in winning souls. He had little doctrinal explanation for his experience and testified only to regeneration. Later, better informed, he was led to seek the witness of the Spirit to entire sanctification as the "second work of grace."

Later, at a holiness convention in Newport, Ky., he received, after a night of prayer, "the unmistakable witness that he was wholly sanctified." Hughes adds, "For the last thirty-seven years I have never seen a day that I have not had the divine assurance that the blood of Jesus

Christ, His Son, cleansed from all sin" (J. W. Hughes, *Autobiography*, p. 96). This, as he later told his bishop, was consistent with his ordination vows, namely, to seek after perfect love until he found it.

The results of God's dealings with J. W. Hughes included pastoral and evangelistic effectiveness, the founding of Central Holiness and Kingswood camp meetings and the founding of Asbury and Kingswood colleges. His influence continues to bless thousands.

85. Lizzy H. Glide (b. 1852)

The name of Mrs. Lizzy H. Glide is preserved, among other places, on the campus of Asbury College and the Glide Memorial Church in San Francisco which has been in the news several times in recent years. Lizzy Snyder was born in Louisiana, a daughter of a medical doctor. Hers was a devout Christian home. She graduated from Greenwood Seminary in Lebanon, Tenn., in 1868. Soon after the Civil War the family moved to Sacramento, Calif., where they united with the Methodist Episcopal Church South. There she met a young rancher by the name of Joseph Glide. They were married in 1871. Her husband became very wealthy as the result of income from his several ranches, and his wife continued to be active in the Methodist church for some 20 years. They lived in the Glide mansion, one of the showplaces of the state capital.

Evangelist Sam Jones held a revival in the Methodist church there, and Mrs. Glide responded to the invitation to consecrate everything to Christ. In her room she made an entire consecration to the Lord and later at a public service she reaffirmed it. This experience of entire sanctification was for her even more epochal than her conversion experience in terms of the consequences. Henceforth, she was dedicated to Christ 100 percent. This led her to a

145

great concern for missionary work at home and abroad. She established a mission in Sacramento which became "a great soul-saving station" (J. C. McPheeters, *Life Story of Lizzy H. Glide* [San Francisco: 1936], p. 11).

For a woman to go from the Glide mansion to the slums seeking to win the lost made a profound impression on the capital. She recognized that what had happened to her was what Wesley described as entire sanctification, and she became an ardent advocate of the experience and the doctrine till her death. She became very dedicated to missions abroad and contributed all that she had available for that purpose.

Her husband died in 1906, leaving his wife his estate, and she had very little business experience. She became a Christian philanthropist, erecting a home for girls in San Francisco and a beautiful dormitory at the University of California in Berkeley named Epworth Hall. Soon after, she visited Asbury College and as a result gave money for the dormitory for girls which is one of the more conspicuous buildings on the campus to this day. As radio became increasingly known, she arranged for Bob Schuler of Los Angeles to be her radio preacher. For years the station was "one of the most powerful voices for righteousness on the Pacific coast" (p. 15).

For many years Mrs. Glide had dreamed of a great evangelistic church in San Francisco ministering to the unchurched masses in the city numbering nearly a half million. Oil was discovered on a Bakersfield ranch, and this added greatly to the Glide Foundation. A strategic lot was secured in San Francisco, and the completed edifice was dedicated by Bishop Arthur Moore in 1931. The fifth anniversary of the church was celebrated at the time when Mrs. Glide was 83 years of age. Adjacent to the church was the Glide Hotel and Apartments. This luxurious hotel was also a temperance hotel giving a Christian testimony to thousands. Dr. J. C. McPheeters was pastor of the church since the beginning and for many years thereafter until called to the full-time presidency of Asbury Theological Seminary.

Bishop James Cannon, Jr., reported that once he and another clergyman asked Mrs. Glide for $5,000 to complete a church in the Pacific conference. She was hesitant for a while but asked questions concerning whether the church was really evangelistic. On being convinced that souls were being saved in the church and the preaching was scriptural, she took her checkbook and wrote a check for $5,000 saying, "I give it because you say that souls are being saved" (p. 107). The remarkable thing about Mrs. Glide was not simply her philanthrophy, but the depth and extent of her consecration. It teaches us that being wealthy is not necessarily bad; it all depends on what one does with the wealth. Mrs. Glide's consecration and testimony to full salvation were made with no reservations.

86. Seth Cook Rees (1854-1933)

Born in a Quaker home on an Indiana farm, Seth Rees (the father of Paul S. Rees, internationally known preacher, author, and lecturer) was a man of exceptional natural and spiritual power. Converted in a Quaker meeting house as a teenager from a life of sin, he was soon effective as a young evangelistic preacher. For years he served as pastor of Friends churches, frequently engaging in evangelistic work at the same time.

Later, he founded the Portsmouth Camp Meeting in Rhode Island, was pastor of the Church of the Nazarene in Pasadena and cofounder of the Pilgrim Holiness church.

The key to his success, as a spiritual giant and an effective soul winner, was what his biographer-son termed "the mighty Baptism with the Holy Ghost and Fire." In the words of Seth Rees himself:

Under ordinary preaching I felt fairly comfortable, and could stand to all the tests put to the congregation. But under the searchlight of the ministry of such men as David B. Updegraff or Dr. Dougan Clark, I would feel keenly conscious of a shortage in my experience. Again and again have I rushed from the meeting into the woods or open country, by day or by night, to weep and cry to God for hours. I really reached a state of conviction, even after I had preached for years, when the wretchedness and anguish of my heart were often inconceivable. My suffering under conviction for inbred sin greatly surpassed anything I endured when an awakened sinner. I had been in the ministry for ten years and, incongruous and presumptuous as it may seem, I had dreamed of places of prominence and honor in my church. To give up my reputation and renounce my ambition for place, and die out completely to what might be said or thought about me, seemed more than I could possibly do.

But the Holy Ghost had "harpooned" me, and I found no rest, day or night, until I gave up entirely. I went on my face before God and lay prostrate before Him, crying for deliverance from the "old man." I longed for human sympathy. I remembered ministers who I thought could help me, but no help came. It was the darkest day I ever saw. After hours of agony I began to be filled with a sense of sinking, sinking, and it seemed as if I was dying. Then I began to say, "Yes," to the Lord. "Yes! Yes! Amen! Amen!" The past, present and future, all the known and all the unknown, my reputation, my all, went into God's lap. I gladly consented to be deposed from the ministry. One of the things that the Holy Ghost brought before me at that time was my future attitude toward the distinctive views of our Society—the Quaker Church. Would I follow Him if it led me contrary to my previous religious teaching? I little knew then what was implied or what it would cost me to make this consecration, but I said "Yes." I "died hard," but I "died sure."

148

At last there began to creep into my soul a tranquil feeling, a holy hush, a death-like stillness, a sweet, placid *"second* rest." I had let go, and He had embraced me in His arms. Eight hours later the conscious filling came, and from that hour I had convictions of certainty. "The old man" was "put off," "the body of sin" was "destroyed," "the old leaven" was "purged out," "the flesh" was "cut away," "the son of the bondwoman" was "excommunicated," "the carnal mind" was "crucified," and I was dead indeed unto sin. He did it. No credit belongs to me. The Holy Ghost came in, cleansed the temple, spread the table, and I took supper with the Father, Son, and Holy Ghost that very day. He settled all my difficulties, expelled all my doubts, metamorphosed my duties into delights, dazzled my head with glory and filled my heart with dancing.

Later he confessed that in contending for the faith he "lost much of the kernel of the *experience* fighting for the *doctrine."* But after that, with added maturity, came a "rest of faith" in which he learned to *trust* as well as obey. His influence for holy living continues to this day. One of his close friends, Dr. H. Orton Wiley, characterized him as "a rugged warrior, an anointed minister, a fiery evangelist, a successful soul winner, a gifted man of God, an earnest Christian."

No greater evangelist ever graced a platform . . . a peculiar unction rested upon him, and his messages so moved the people that oftentimes great congregations were swayed by the power of his Spirit-anointed oratory.

(See Paul S. Rees, *Seth Cook Rees, The Warrior-Saint* [Indianapolis, Ind.: Pilgrim Book Room, 1934].)

87. **Joseph H. Smith** (1855-1946)

The testimony of Joseph H. Smith to the "second blessing" is given in the following words, 63 years after that blessed event.

The very night of my conversion there was placed in my hand a copy of J. A. Wood's book on *Perfect Love*. The eager appetite of my new life set me to devouring its contents, and I read until long after midnight . . .

Then all the ardor of my first love was spent in pursuit of holiness . . . Nearly five weeks had passed; when I told the Lord that I did not know how to get it, and asked him these four questions: Will I pray more? Will I study more? Will I fast more? Will I pay more?

Just then the Spirit used a little home incident to cross out for me all those big "I's" and showed me it was nothing that I could do but that he who had let me in out of the dark and cold would himself lift me up to the rest that remains to the people of God. That was a Friday night. All day Saturday over a busy desk I was looking up—Sabbath in six usual services, I was still looking up.

Monday morning, early at the office, I supplied what had been missing from my prayer hitherto and said, "Lord, wilt thou lift me up now?" And he sweetly answered, "I will, my child." Faith at once embraced my cleansing through the Blood. The Holy Spirit came closer and entered more deeply than before, and gently announced, "I am come to abide." That Monday night, in a general testimony meeting at the church, I witnessed to the occurrence and stated that my joys today have been as much beyond those of the last five weeks as those were greater than all the pleasures I had in the world.

88. Henry Clay Morrison (1857-1942)

Henry Clay Morrison, Methodist evangelist, founder of Asbury Theological Seminary, was born and raised on a farm near Glasgow, Ky. His parents were God-fearing Methodists. Their neighbors were predominantly Baptists and Methodists and often cooperated in special revival services. As a child he was often under conviction for such sins as going with some of the boys for a walk in the woods on Sunday afternoon. At one revival meeting Henry sat up close to the front, hoping that someone would personally speak to him about seeking the Lord, but no one did. Afterwards he was tempted to enter into a life of outward sin just to get attention since he had been ignored when he felt his need of Christ. Then he concluded that he had "sinned away his day of grace." More than once he joined other sinners at the mourners' bench where he prayed during the service.

Just as he was about to conclude that his situation was hopeless, a Baptist neighbor said, "God is not mad at you; God loves you." This struck home and with a leap of faith he experienced the joy of sins forgiven. He was then 13 years of age. Later he was baptized in the creek, joined the Methodist church, and initiated family prayers in his home.

Shortly after that he felt the call to preach. He became an effective debater and preacher. As a pastor, he had numerous calls to conduct revival meetings. One of them occurred in Winchester, Ky., in 1887 when 150 professed conversion. This led to many additions to church membership, the organization of a Young Men's Christian Association, and the stimulus for moving Kentucky Wesleyan College from Millersburg to Winchester in 1890. While evangelist at Paris, Ky., attendance outgrew the Methodist church, the courthouse, and the large Presbyterian church. Large trains were run from Lexington to Paris for those attending the meetings.

The great crisis in Morrison's personal life was light on the experience of entire sanctification. Only two clergymen in the Kentucky Conference, W. B. Godbey and John S. Keene, professed to have received the experience of perfect love. Morrison was prejudiced against the doctrine largely because of erroneous ideas concerning it. However, two of his associates, W. S. Grinstead and Horace Cockarill, stimulated a desire for a deeper work of grace. Both had themselves experienced the work of entire sanctification and urged Morrison to enter in.

While Morrison was assisting in a revival meeting, a letter from his friend Cockarill enabled him to grasp the full significance of this experience. He was convinced that the doctrine was true, that this was God's free gift for him, and that he must have it. During prayer in his room with Dr. J. A. Young he was convinced that the power of God was in the community and in the room. In his words,

> Instantly, the Spirit fell upon me and I fell backwards upon the divan, as helpless as a dead man. I was conscious of the mighty hand of God dealing with me. Dr. Young leaped up, caught me in his arms, and called me again and again but I was powerless to answer. Just as I came to myself and recovered the use of my limbs, a round ball of liquid fire seemed to strike me in the face, dissolve, and enter into me. I leaped up and shouted aloud, "Glory to God." Dr. Young, who still had me in his arms, threw me back on the divan and said, "Morrison, what do you mean, you frightened me; I thought you were dying. Why did you act that way?" "I did not do anything, Doctor," said I, "the Lord did it." I rose and walked the floor feeling light as a feather. (P. A. Wesche, *Henry Clay Morrison, Crusader, Saint* [Herald Press, 1963], p. 44)

After this Morrison declined to testify to it, fearing it would be misunderstood. While pastor in Danville, Ky., he was bemoaning his lost sense of cleansing so deeply, that sometimes sleep fled from him. The Presbyterian minister residing in Danville advised the distressed Methodist pastor:

> My young brother, the Lord has not forsaken you, but is leading you into what Mr. Wesley called Christian perfection. The Baptists call it the rest of faith, the Presbyterians a higher life in the fullness of the Spirit.

The Presbyterian minister went on to report how he had received his personal Pentecost when he was pastor in Louisville. Not long after, while Morrison was reading from Revelation, "As many as I love . . . I chasten," the light broke in upon him. Said he,

> It seemed as if Jesus spoke the words from his own lips, and my heart was filled with peace and joy. Again for want of instruction I failed to testify, lost my full assurance, and had a conflict more or less severe for many months before I became fully established. (p. 46)

This was in 1888, but shortly after, Morrison not only professed the experience himself but to the end of his life became a most vigorous advocate of what John Wesley and the earlier John, the apostle, called "perfect love."

89. C. T. Studd (1860-1931)

C. T. Studd, pioneer missionary to the heart of Africa, learned by experience that it is not sufficient to get people converted to Christ. He found it impossible to promote true evangelism without true holiness. He remembered the words of Booth-Tucker in China, "Remember that mere soul saving is comparatively easy work, and it is not nearly so important as that of manufacturing the saved ones into saints, soldiers, and saviours." After the first eager response to the gospel in central Africa there was evidence of carnality among the converts and even among the leading Christians and evangelists. It was manifested in self-seeking, unwillingness to live sacrificially, criticism, and slothfulness. Studd prayed about it, searched the Word, talked about it, and wrote:

> Christ came to save us by his blood and by his Spirit, blood to wash away our past sins, Spirit to change our hearts and empower us to live right. He came not to save us in our sins but from them. Christ

did not die to whitewash us, he died to re-create us and none but his re-creations enter heaven.

Both at home and on the field the crucial period is described by Studd's biographer as the wilderness experience in which those led out of bondage fell to quarrelling and complaining instead of going on to the conquest of evil within and without. At length Studd, with a few other missionaries, covenanted together to go all the way, to die out to the self-life, and, with the reckless abandon of a charging infantryman, to be utterly yielded to the Holy Spirit. From these the holy fire spread over the entire work, and others entered into the life of full consecration and the baptism with the Holy Ghost. The Worldwide Evangelization Crusade has holiness of heart and life as a major emphasis as a result of learning by experience that anything less is inadequate for the evangelization of the world. Studd represents a masculine kind of saintliness. His colaborer said of him, "From him I learned that God's ideal of a saint is not a man primarily concerned with his own sanctification. God's saint is fifty percent a soldier" (N. P. Grubb, *C. T. Studd, Athlete and Pioneer*).

90. Samuel Logan Brengle (1860-1936)

Col. Samuel Logan Brengle, in *Helps to Holiness*, testifies that for years he sought the experience of heart purity at intervals until the revelation came that he must stir himself up to take hold of God (Isa. 64:7). Thereafter he sought God "feeling or no feeling." He soon discovered that self (pride and spiritual ambition) was keeping him away from the blessing. When he confessed the sin of pride and crucified the self-life, he was able to appropriate the promise that "if we confess . . . he [will] cleanse" (1 John 1:9). He relates, "In that instant 'the blood of Christ, who through the Eternal Spirit offered himself without spot to

154

God, purged my conscience from dead works to serve the living God'" (see Heb. 9:14). From that time he began to testify to the experience and to preach it in his pulpit. The effect was profound, and others felt their need of a similar experience. He continued to put himself on record, to take up his cross daily, and to walk softly and expectantly with God. A few days later, upon arising he said, "He that believeth on me, though he were dead, yet shall he live." As he expresses it,

> The Holy Ghost, the other "Comforter," was in those words, and in an instant my soul melted before the Lord like I was before the fire, and I knew Jesus. He was revealed in me as he had promised, and I loved him with an unutterable love. I wept and adored; and loved, and loved and loved . . . That experience fixed my theology. From then till now men and devils might as well try to get me to question the presence of the sun in the heavens as to question the existence of God, the divinity of Jesus Christ, and the sanctifying power of an ever present Almighty Holy Spirit.

91. Reuben (Bud) Robinson (1860-1942)

"Uncle Bud" Robinson, as he was affectionately known, was one of the most unique and effective evangelists America has ever known. Born in eastern Tennessee in extreme poverty, his widowed mother with several of her 13 children moved to Texas and her illiterate son, Bud, became a ranch-hand at the age of 16. Soon after his conversion, even before he could read or write, he was called to preach. His long and effective evangelistic ministry, the handicaps he overcame, and his witticisms endeared him to the hearts of thousands.

To the Texas ranch with its wicked cowboys there came a Methodist circuit rider. His prayers and exhortations made a deep impression on Robinson, then 20 years of age. Soon after, at a camp meeting he was struck with deep conviction of his sins and after wrestling at an altar of prayer he was converted while they were praying. In his words, "The bottom of heaven dropped out and my soul was flooded with light and joy until literal waves of glory rolled up and down my soul" (*Life,* p. 30). That same night while trying to sleep under a wagon he received his call to preach. On August 11, 1880, he was "born again" and called to preach the gospel.

Six years later, after Bud had preached with great effectiveness, Dr. W. B. Godbey came from Kentucky to Texas with a message of perfect love or entire sanctification. Robinson decided, "That is the best religion that I ever heard a man preach and I will have it or die" (*Life,* p. 48). Bud Robinson sought secretly for this experience for two years. Then he began to preach it for two more years while admitting he did not have the blessing. He urged others to join him in seeking God's fullness. After 10 years of intense seeking and preaching, his agony became so intense that he felt holiness of heart indispensable. After preaching on a Sunday on this subject, he stopped cultivating his corn field the next Monday morning and prayed again. In his words, "I had begun to seek this blessing in 1886 and now it was June 2, 1890 . . . I had often consecrated all that I had . . . but that did not bring the victory . . . I could hear the Lord say 'If everything else goes then I will stay with you.' I said, Lord, let everything else go. Then I had that strong peculiar feeling that God was so close to me that my soul trembled in God's presence and it seemed that God kindled up a fire in the very bottom of my heart . . . When my heart was emptied of anger, pride, jealousy, and envy, then it seemed that a river of peace broke loose from the clouds . . . until the waves of heaven became so great and grand and glorious that it seemed to me that I would die if God did not stay his hand" (*Life*, pp. 53, 54). For three hours (from nine until noon) he was overflowing with the joy of the Lord. He testified to his mother that noon and a few years later she also found the same experience of the Spirit-filled life.

With his characteristic metaphorical language, Uncle Bud dramatized his religious experiences without losing his simple sincerity. This lends a note of authenticity to his witness. Forty years and millions of miles and sermons later he bore witness to the same truth of entire sanctification.

92. C. W. Ruth (1865-1941)

Born in Bucks County, Pennsylvania, southeast of Allentown, of devout Christian parents of the Evangelical Association, C. W. Ruth was exposed to Christian influences from childhood. Although with meager formal education he was called to preach while working in an Indianapolis printing office. During his ministry of more than four decades as pastor and evangelist he saw more than 30,000 seek God for pardon or purity. Much of his ministry was within the Church of the Nazarene but his influence extended far outside this membership, within and without the holiness movement. He was also an effective writer. One of his books, provided by a Free Methodist pastor, was used to bring this writer to the experience of entire sanctification. Ruth describes his own experience of two "works of grace" in these words:

> Conviction became so pungent and intense, I publicly confessed myself a seeker; after much earnest crying and agonizing prayer to God, by day and night, confessing my sins, I was gloriously converted on the following Sunday night. The pastor of the church I attended, after an earnest sermon, invited seekers to come forward to the altar of prayer. I rejoiced in the opportunity, and rushed forward to the altar, fell upon

my knees, and pleaded for mercy. At about 9:30 o'clock, God in mercy heard my prayer, the burden of my guilt was rolled away, the light of heaven broke into my soul, the Spirit witnessed with my spirit that I was pardoned and accepted by God, and was indeed a new creature in Christ. Although I had been averse to religious demonstrations, I now found myself shouting aloud the praises of God. I was born again and I knew it. This occurred early in September, 1882. Praise God forever more! Soon after this I was baptized and united with the church.

During the following year I lived a most earnest and devoted Christian life, attending faithfully all the means of grace. I carried two testaments—one German and one English—in my pockets, and used my spare time in studying the same. Thus I maintained a clear justified experience.

But I had gone only a very short time in my Christian experience until I discovered, much to my amazement, that there still remained a something in my heart that hindered me, and at times even defeated me. The principal manifestations of that "something" were, a man-fearing spirit, the uprising of an unholy temper, difficulty in forgiving and loving an enemy, etc. I learned that Jesus could remove the root of those difficulties out of the heart. Just one year after I had been so gloriously converted, while yet in my first love, I definitely sought the experience of entire sanctification. After seeking earnestly for some days, one Sunday night while walking down the sidewalk toward the church conscious that I had consecrated my all for time and eternity, I was enabled to look up into heaven, and say, "I believe that the blood of Jesus cleanseth my heart from all sin now; he sanctifies me now," and suddenly and consciously the Holy Ghost fell upon me, and I knew just as positively and as assuredly that God had sanctified me through and through, as I had known a year before that he had pardoned my sins. I rushed into the church, and before the pastor had time to announce the opening hymn, I told the congregation what had occurred on the sidewalk, and that God had sanctified me wholly. Billows of glory swept over me until my joy seemed to be utterly inexpressible and uncontainable. Oh, the blessedness of that hour! Surely heaven could be no better. And from that day to the present—now almost twenty years —Satan has never had the audacity to tempt me to doubt even for one minute that God did not then and there sanctify me wholly.

93. Charles Elmer Cowman (1868-1924)

Rev. Charles Cowman, founder of the Oriental Missionary Society, lived an intense life of dedication to missions. Born in Illinois and reared in Iowa on a farm, he moved at the age of 15 to become a telegraph operator. Later, in Chicago, at the age of 21 he was soundly converted to Christ. He then, with no formal religious training, became an effective soul winner, using personal evangelism.

However, as zealous and effective as he was, a spiritual need was discovered. A layman, George Semister, often told Cowman of a "wonderful blessing" he had himself received and urged Cowman to seek the same. Charles felt no need of anything further. A sudden outburst of anger revealed his need of patience. Immediately he asked forgiveness and with the counsel and prayers of Semister confessed his indwelling sin and need of entire sanctification. As Charles Cowman recalled these moments:

"I was profoundly impressed and powerfully sustained, almost absorbed by the Word. 'This is the will of God, even your sanctification.' 'He that willeth to do His will shall know of the doctrine.' These words cannot be too deeply engraved upon the heart. I will ever seek to have my will one with the will of God." Soon after this self-dedication he added, "I have committed myself and my all into God's hands, and He has accepted the offering. Life henceforth can never be the same."

What was the result? As his biographer put it, "He came into a fresh experience, a second definite work of grace—a crisis as radical and revolutionary as the crisis of regeneration . . . a new power marked his service from that day." "Those who knew him before and after this experience could not question that he had found a new secret of power for his own life and work." (*Charles E. Cowman: Missionary Warrior*, pp. 72-73)

After this he was called repeatedly to churches to report on his success at soul winning in the telegraph offices. This layman with no formal training for the task was soon helping pastors as well as laymen to find the experience in Christ that made them whole and henceforth effective. A call to a missionary career followed which led to service in Japan and Korea and eventually to China.

Today O.M.S. International is a major independent faith mission witnessing effectively in five continents. This is because one layman followed Christ from conversion through cleansing to service.

94. Oswald Chambers (1874-1917)

Another witness is Oswald Chambers, well known to the Christian world for his unique messages on the "deep things of God." This is his personal testimony.

> After I was born again, as a boy, I enjoyed the presence of Jesus Christ wonderfully, but years passed before I gave myself up thoroughly to His work. Later I was in college, and a servant of God came there and spoke about the Holy Spirit. I determined that I would get all that there was going, and I went to my room and asked God as simply and as definitely as I could for the baptism of the Holy Spirit, whatever that meant.
>
> From that day for four years nothing but the over-ruling grace of God and the kindness of friends kept me out of an asylum. God used me during those four years

160

in the conversion of souls, but I had no conscious communion with Him. The Bible was the dullest, most uninteresting book in existence. I see now that was God taking me through every ramification of my being by the light of the Holy Spirit and His Word. The last three months of that four years things reached a climax. I was getting very, very desperate. I knew no one had what I wanted; but I knew that if what I presently had was all the Christianity there was, the thing was a fraud.

Luke 11:13 got hold of me. Had I asked definitely for the Holy Spirit when I was as bad-motivated as I was? Then this was borne in on me that I had to claim this gift from God on the testimony of Jesus Christ and testify to it. But the thought came: If you testify and claim the gift of the Holy Spirit on the word of Jesus Christ, God will make it known to those who know you best (and they thought I was an angel) how bad you are in your heart. I was not willing to be a fool for Jesus Christ's sake.

There was a little meeting held in Dunoon; I was surrounded by Christian workers who knew me well. A well-known lady worker was asked to take the after-meeting. She did not speak; she put us all to prayer and then sang, "Touch me again, Lord." I rose to my feet. I had no feeling, no vision of God, but this sheer, dogged determination to take Him at His word, to put this thing to the final test. I stood up and said that . . . and then and there claimed the gift of the Holy Spirit in dogged committal on Luke 11:13. I had no vision of heaven, no vision of angels; I had nothing. I was dry and empty. Then the verse that came to me during that condition was this: "You shall receive power, after that the Holy Ghost is come upon you." But I had no power, no realization of God, no witness of the Holy Spirit.

Two days afterwards I was asked to speak at a meeting. I spoke, as empty and as dry as a trumpet, but forty souls came out to the front. Did I praise God? No, I was terrified and left them and went back; I went to an old servant of God and told him what had happened. What do you think he said to me: "My

161

dear young fellow, don't you remember claiming on the word of Jesus Christ the Holy Spirit as a gift, and He said that you should receive power after that the Holy Ghost came upon you? That is the power."

Like a flash something happened inside me, and I saw that I had been wanting power in my own fist to show people and say: "Look what I have; you see what I have gotten by putting my all on the altar." If the four years previously were hell on earth those following have been truly heaven on earth. I do thank God from the bottom of my heart for this. In Acts 2:4 it says: "They were all filled with the Holy Ghost." Glory be to God, the last aching abyss of the human heart is filled to overflowing with the love of God.

If you read II Corinthians 4 you see the apostle Paul's message there: "For we preach not ourselves, but Jesus Christ as Lord: and ourselves your servants for Jesus' sake." Love is the beginning, love is the middle, and love is the end. You know what He does when He comes in. He takes out that old carnal nature root and branch and ramification, and lives inside. And who do you think you see afterwards?

> Jesus only, Jesus ever,
>   Jesus all in all we sing;
> Saviour, Sanctifier, Healer,
>   Glorious Lord and coming King.

Oh, that the Omnipotent God would grant that everyone would have stripped from them the veil that the prince of this world has put on and could see the marvellous freedom God brings. Not myself, but my Master; not my introspective self, but Jesus only.

95. Charles Ewing Brown (1883-1971)

The former editor of the *Gospel Trumpet* and lecturer in theology, Charles Ewing Brown, in Anderson Theological Seminary, wrote thus:

There came a swift, miraculous spiritual summer to our community in which my infidel, drunken father was converted. I followed him in a few days; some

162

months later my mother entered into the fellowship of the faith.

Our spiritual leader did not tarry long. He taught the doctrine of entire sanctification. I began to pray earnestly and seek for that blessing. I felt such a burden of yearning on my heart that I can remember it yet as a pain, a longing, a cry to God. I fasted for some time.

The greatest trouble I had in seeking sanctification was what I found later to be the major infirmity of the modern soul—doubt. No scientist in his laboratory, or scholar in his study, has ever pressed closer to the chilling doubt of the reality of the spiritual life than I pressed as I knelt on the ground amid the awakening grass and the budding flowers, while I sought to see the throne of the Eternal in the bushes as Moses found it so many years ago.

Down on my knees in the orchard at the foot of the hill, in an agony of yearning desire and struggle with doubt, I pressed along the road trampled by Elijah when he heard the strong wind, but God was not in the wind. He felt a mighty earthquake, but God was not in the earthquake. After the earthquake, a fire, but the Lord was not in the fire. And after the fire, a still, small voice.

There in the silence, with only the winds rustling the grass and the trees, the thunders of eternity came to me from the distance as a soft whisper of God:

It is done. This is Pentecost. This is the baptism of the Holy Spirit. This is fire and lightning and healing power. This is heart purity. This is fellowship with the gentle Jesus, the country Preacher who loved children; and this is the call to go and minister the healing of His word and works wherever you can help others.

It has been a long time since I heard the whisper of Jesus in the old orchard on the hillside. Since then the days have stretched into years, and the years have passed into decades, and I have carried His healing message to men of nearly every race and kind around the world.

96. James Blaine Chapman (1884-1947)

Dr. Chapman is remembered as one of the founding fathers of the Church of the Nazarene and as one of her most exemplary leaders. The home which he knew as a child was not a Christian home. Although his parents were good, moral people they made no professions of Christian faith. However, young "Jimmie" had a tender conscience and more than once was touched by an occasional Christian witness: the man who inquired if any of the family belonged to any church, the new convert who was heard singing a gospel song as he passed by.

While a teenager his parents moved from their farm in south central Illinois to Oklahoma. There, not far from Oklahoma City, were more sinners and also more saints than in their Illinois environs. Here for the first time he heard a sermon by a holiness preacher (Rev. Albright of the United Brethren church). He listened in silence to a layman who dutifuly witnessed of his faith to young Jimmie. Not long after, he attended a nearby holiness camp meeting and listened night after night to sermons which seemed directed specifically to him. The congregational singing was so fervent that he realized they had something he lacked and needed. After being an appreciative listener in several services he went forward to pray at the altar. He seemed to be at the edge of a precipice. After he took the "plunge" by faith, assurance of God's pardon came at once. He arose to say, "I am a Christian."

On the evening of the day after his new birth, he was encouraged to seek entire sanctification as a preventive against his love growing lukewarm. He again sought the Lord not for pardon but for a "clean heart." He said yes to everything that might hinder a full acceptance by Christ. After praying for about an hour and yielding everything known and unknown to God he trusted "for the sanctifying fullness of the Holy Spirit," as he later expressed it. With this came the assurance of acceptance and cleansing so convincing that he sought "no external token at all."

One year later, at the age of 16 while preaching, he sensed an unusual measure of the Spirit's unction, and with it came the needed assurance that his was a call to the gospel ministry. Later, he recalled a simple and beautiful poem expressive of the author's experience as well as his own:

> I've entered the vale of the sweet Beulah land,
>> Jesus satisfies me.
> I'm walking with Jesus, I'm led by His hand,
>> Jesus satisfies me.

In his mature years, as a writer, his biographer reports, "Paramount in the written message of Dr. Chapman was the emphasis on entire sanctification as a second crisis experience in Christian life, the Wesleyan doctrinal emphasis" (Corlett, *Spirit Filled,* p. 107).

Years later Dr. Chapman wrote,

> The thing of which I boast today is that when I came to Jesus as a lad of fifteen He touched me in pardoning mercy and made me know I was His own. When I came in full consecration He touched me in cleansing fullness and gave me a pure heart, and He has touched me with frequent assurances all down through these years since the time when I knew Him first. This is my solemn testimony.

And the witness of James Blaine Chapman continues today in memory, in his writings, and the institutions he did so much to influence, to the enrichment of us all. All that he did for God in many years of service had its origin in what God did in him as a teenager.

97. Harry E. Jessop (1884-1974)

The former president of Chicago Evangelistic Institute, author of *Foundations of Doctrine* and *I Met a Man with a Shining Face,* testifies thus:

From that first moment of the realization of saving grace, I wanted all that God could give me. It was not long before I began to feel that, glorious as my new experience in conversion had been, God was now holding before me something of a deeper nature than that which I already enjoyed.

While my love for Christ was such that it pained me to know that I had grieved Him, my spiritual life was far from constant and my communion was not sustained. I was conscious of a lack of power in service and of a strange inward conflict which did not seem to be consistent with New Testament standards.

One day, however, an unexpected thing happened. I met a man whose face shone with something I had never seen before. It was a heavenly radiance betokening a real soul satisfaction and suggesting a deep inward rest. As I looked at him, my heart was filled with an unspeakable longing to have what he possessed. But the longer I looked, the more puzzled I became.

As he looked at me, he evidently read the longing of my hungry heart, for he startled me with a strange question: "Brother," said he, "have *you* been baptized with the Holy Ghost and with fire?"

My reply must have sounded simple, but it came from my heart as I answered: "I don't know what you mean by being baptized with the Holy Ghost and fire, but if that is it that shines out of your face, I want it."

He was not long in telling me that the radiance on his countenance was the result of a definite spiritual experience, a baptism with the Holy Spirit. Wesley called it the Second Blessing. "This," said my newfound friend, "is for *you,* and for every child of God who will seek it today."

He began to give me some simple instructions as to how I might receive it, showing me the need of a complete consecration, my entire life with all it reaches being demanded as a living sacrifice to God. When that consecration was complete, a simple act of faith would bring the blessing.

It is a joy to testify that the consecration was made and the faith exercised; and, blessed be God, the blessing came!

There have been definite results, both immediate and abiding. The phases have been many. Here, however, I shall mention only three.

First of all, with this baptism with the Holy Spirit, there came a consciousness of *deep inward cleansing. . . .*

. . . second feature of this experience was a *deep sense of release.* You will notice that again I am using that word *deep*, for that is exactly what it was—deeper down than anything I had before known.

It seemed to reach the very depths of my being. Inward bonds were broken and fetters snapped, so that whereas there had been a measure of bondage to people, their opinions and views, there was now a glorious liberty in the service of God and in the doing of His will.

A further result of this spiritual baptism has been a *deep inward illumination.* The light seemed to break away down in the inner recesses of my being. It was as though subterranean passages, hitherto dark and unexplored, had been suddenly lighted up and their darkness chased out by a divine glory which surged through them.

Of the abiding peace, the power for service, the periods of exultant joy and so many other glorious accompaniments, time forbids me to speak, except to say that every day the marvel grows as to why the Lord should have been so good to me.

98. **E. Stanley Jones** (1884-1973)

The testimony to full redemption which one of the most influential leaders of the modern world bears, puts the familiar biblical and Wesleyan concepts in the phraseology of modern thought. Dr. E. Stanley Jones thus testifies in *The Meaning of Sanctification*, by C. E. Brown (The Warner Press, 1946):

> I came to Christ bankrupt. My capacity to blunder drove me to his feet, and to my astonishment he took me, forgave me, and sent my happy soul singing its way down the years. . . .
>
> I walked in the joy of that for months and then the clouds began to gather. There was something within me not redeemed, something else down in the cellar that seemed to be sullenly at war with this new life. I was at war with myself.
>
> I think I can see what happened. We live in two minds—the conscious and the subconscious. . . .
>
> Into the conscious mind there is introduced at conversion a new life, a new loyalty, a new love. But the subconscious mind does not obey this new life. Its driving instincts drive for fulfillment apart from any morality built up in the conscious mind. There ensues a clash between the new life in the conscious mind and the instinct of the subconscious. The house of man-soul becomes a house divided against itself.
>
> I wondered if this was the best that Christianity could be—to leave one in this divided condition? I found to my glad surprise the teaching concerning the Holy Spirit, and I found the area of the work of the Holy Spirit largely, if not entirely, in the subconscious. I found that if I would surrender to the Holy Spirit this conscious mind—all I knew and all I did not know—he would cleanse at these depths I could not control.
>
> I surrendered and accepted the gift by faith. He did cleanse as a refining fire. In that cleansing there was a unifying. Conscious and subconscious minds were brought under a single control and redemption. That control was the Holy Spirit. I was no longer at war with myself. Life was on a permanently higher level. It was no longer up and down. The soul had caught its stride. I went on my way singing a new song. That song has continued. It is fresher today than then.

99. William Edwin Sangster (1900-1960)

Dr. Sangster's son has written an excellent biography giving a relatively objective and yet intimate view of this pastor, scholar, saint. Dr. Sangster is best known as past president of the Wesleyan Conference in England and for many years as pastor of perhaps Methodism's most influential pulpit, that is Westminster Central Hall. As a boy he was the admirer of heroes beginning with Admiral Nelson. After his conversion he became increasingly interested in the lives of the saints. He was ecumenical, appreciating the heroes of the faith in different communions, but he especially admired John Wesley for his life and for his work.

Dr. Sangster's lifelong pursuit of holiness was influenced to a large extent by John Wesley. Always, however, his quest was Christ-centered, and he constantly recognized the importance of a moment-by-moment relation to Christ rather than relying on what was done in one climactic moment. In his case, faith and dedication together with his native talents made him a very effective force for the evangelical cause in the British Isles and in English-speaking countries from the United States to Australia. Like John Wesley he was reticent about testifying to a specific experience which he called entire sanctification. His stress, rather, was on the constant openness to the leading of God and to effectiveness in service for the Master.

During the air raids of World War II in London, the basement of Westminster Hall was an air raid shelter. Here Dr. Sangster ministered to "all sorts of conditions of men" living with them in this subterranean retreat. After he had ministered to their several needs, he would reserve a vigil after midnight in which he worked on a book entitled *The Path to Perfection*. This was a study of John

Wesley's doctrine of the subject of entire sanctification, a volume which had a wide influence and was accepted as a dissertation for a doctor's degree at the University of London.

This is a volume which influenced my own doctoral labors at Harvard, a book with which I often disagreed. It was Dr. Sangster who reviewed my doctoral dissertation published as *The More Excellent Way* (1952), a review very commendatory in nature which appeared in *Religion and Life*. I was privileged to hear Dr. Sangster preach in Westminster Hall in December, 1953. After presenting myself, he embraced me as a beloved brother in the Lord. I was impressed with his ability to concentrate on one person as if he were the only one in the world who mattered.

100. Julian C. McPheeters (1889-   )

Dr. Julian Claudius McPheeters, United Methodist pastor-evangelist and president emeritus of Asbury Theological Seminary, was converted at the age of five. After typical stresses of the teenage years he was in college, pondering his vocation for life. In his own words:

> My sophomore year I was wrestling with this matter of what I was going to do. I wanted to be a lawyer; I was a debater and took on all comers. . . . But God was talking with me. In those days . . . a cousin came from college, a ministerial candidate, and I watched his life. I worked with him in a factory; and it was that summer, when I was intimately associated with this cousin . . . during his vacation, that I decided to enter the ministry. His life was a deciding factor with me and I have never regretted that decision.
>
> Following that crisis, the next crisis . . . was when I went away to a small church college in Missouri. There I ran across a young man who had come over from Asbury College. He was a little different stripe. This

boy's name was Greene and he would say, "Amen," in chapel at times. We never heard that in our school, but we thought a lot of this young fellow. We would whisper around quietly among ourselves, "He is a good fellow, but he is awfully religious." Greene returned from his circuit one Monday and told me, "I have met the most wonderful woman on the way down on the train, and she has had a wonderful experience. I have made arrangements for you and Jack Wright [that was my roommate] to go down to Sister Winter's and meet this good woman."

We were having a revival, a college revival, in the Methodist church; and this dear woman was first deaconess of the former Methodist church, then retired. Her hair was gray but her face was radiant and young. She had heard about the college revival and, at her own expense, came from St. Louis, about 150 miles distance, just to hold prayer meetings. We went that evening before the church service; only we three college boys went to see this lady. I looked in the face of this very wonderful woman and saw a shine and radiance upon her countenance that convinced me, "She has something that you do not have." It was beautiful to look into her face.

She asked me, "Do you believe in sanctification?"

I replied, "I don't know whether I believe in sanctification or not; you'll have to tell me what you mean." She told about a life of abounding love for God's children, a completeness of victory, loving God supremely and loving your neighbor as yourself, a life of love and of great victory. That appealed to me. I said in my heart, "I like that." She went on talking and unfolding the Scriptures to me in a wonderful way, and then she paused. I inquired, "Is that all there is?"

She affirmed, "That's it."

I told her, "Well, I will take that right now." While she was talking, something said to me, "Would you be willing to say, 'Amen,' in chapel like Greene and have the people talking about you and saying, 'McPheeters is a good student, but he is off a little'?" I answered back immediately, "Yes, Lord. I will say, 'Amen,' in chapel; I will even say, 'Hallelujah,' if You want me to." And then something happened in my heart; I assured dear Mrs. Skinner, "I take that now."

She got up out of her chair and started to cross the room and she said, "Do you believe that Jesus sanctifies you?"

I said, "Yes, I do." When I said it, I clapped my hands and said, "Glory." It was the first time I had ever said, "Glory," in my life. Well, as an adult I have been saying, "Glory," ever since and have been trying to get as many other people to say, "Glory," also in this life of victory. Sure enough it was a test; in chapel shortly afterwards, the president made a good point and I said, "Amen." The students all looked around.

As could be expected, in a few days one of my good friends, who later became the president of the University of Mexico, said to me, "McPheeters, we think a lot of you, and you are one of our best students; but since you have entered into this experience you call 'sanctification,' some of us have been a bit concerned about you. We feel that you have gotten a little bit off, and we want you to know that we are your friends, and we believe that you are going to be your old self again."

The truth is, I never did recover. And, it has been getting better all through the years. Now as I walk the eventide of life at four score years, and five, I can say it is better than ever, and it is a life of glory to glory, from victory to victory, from triumph to triumph. (Taped from a personal interview with G. A. Turner ca. 1976)

BIBLIOGRAPHY

Arminian Magazine, Aug., 1872.

Asbury, Francis. *The Heart of Asbury's Journal.* Cincinnati: Jennings & Graham, 1904.

Boardman, William Edwin. *The Higher Christian Life.* Boston: Henry Hoyt, 1871.

Brengle, Samuel Logan. *Helps to Holiness.* New York: Salvation Army Printing and Publishing House, 1911.

Brickley, Donald P. *Man of the Morning.* Kansas City: Nazarene Publishing House, 1960.

Brown, C. W. *The Meaning of Sanctification.* Anderson, Ind.: Warner Press, 1945.

Carradine, Beverly. *Sanctification.* Introduction by Rev. L. L. Pickett. Nashville: Publishing House of the M. E. Church, South, Barbee & Smith, Agents, 1891.

Chalmers, Thomas. *The Works of Thomas Chalmers.* 25 vols. Glasgow: W. Collins, 1842.

Cowman, Lettie (Bord). *Charles E. Cowman: Missionary Warrior.* Los Angeles: Oriental Missionary Society, 1928.

Day, Richard Ellsworth. *Bush Aglow: The Life Story of Dwight Lyman Moody, Commoner of Northfield.* Philadelphia: Judson Press, 1936.

Edwards, Jonathan. "Conversion and Experience of President Edwards." Doctrinal Tract No. 18. Boston: Congregational Board of Publication, n.d.

Fox, George. *Journal.* Philadelphia: n.p., n.d.

Garrison, S. O., ed. *Forty Witnesses.* Freeport, Pa.: Fountain Press, 1955.

Godbey, William B. *Autobiography of Rev. W. B. Godbey.* Cincinnati: God's Revivalist Office, 1909.

Gordon, Adoniram Judson. *The Two-fold Life: Or, Christ's Work for Us and Christ's Work in Us.* Boston: H. Gannet, 1884.

Gordon, Ernest Barron. *Adoniram Judson Gordon: A Biography with Letters and Illustrative Extracts Drawn from Un-*

published or Uncollected Sermons and Addresses. New York: Revell Co., 1896.

Grubb, Norman Percy. *C. T. Studd: Athlete and Pioneer.* Grand Rapids: Zondervan, 1941.

Guide to Holiness. Boston and New York.

Hoss, E. E. *William McKendree: A Biographical Study.* Nashville: Cokesbury Press, 1916.

Hughes, John Wesley. *Autobiography of John Wesley Hughes: Founder of Asbury and Kingswood Colleges.* Louisville: Pentecostal Publishing Co., 1923.

Jackson, Thomas, ed. *Lives of Early Methodist Preachers: Chiefly Written by Themselves.* 6 vols. London: Wesleyan Conference Office, 1871-73.

Jessop, Harry Edward. *Foundations of Doctrine in Scripture and Experience: A Student's Handbook on Holiness.* Chicago: Chicago Evangelistic Institute, 1938.

————. *I Met a Man with a Shining Face: An Autobiography in the Things of God.* Winona Lake, Ind.: Light and Life Press, 1956.

King, D. S. *The Riches of Grace or the Blessing of Perfect Love.* Auburn, N.Y.: Wm. J. Moses, 1855.

Lake, Kirsopp, ed. *Apostolic Fathers.* 2 vols. Loeb Classical Library. New York: G. P. Putnam, 1930.

Lawson, J. C. *Deeper Experiences of Famous Christians.* Chicago: Glad Tidings, 1911.

McDonald, William. *The Advocate of Bible Holiness.* n.p., January, 1882.

————. *The New Testament Standard of Piety: or, Love Made Perfect.* Chicago: Christian Witness Co., 1882.

McLeister, Mrs. Clara. *Men and Women of Deep Piety.* Edited by E. E. Shelhamer. Syracuse, N.Y.: Wesleyan Methodist Publishing Association, 1920.

McPheeters, Julius Claudius. *Life Story of Lizzy H. Glide.* San Francisco: Eagle Printing Co., 1936.

Mahan, Asa. *The Baptism of the Holy Ghost.* New York: G. Hughes, 1870.

Marshall, Walter. *The Gospel Mystery of Sanctification Opened.* New York: Southwick and Pelsue, 1811.

Palmer, Walter Clark. *Life and Letters of Leonidas L. Hamline.* New York: Carlton & Porter, 1866.

Pike, John. "How I Was Fully Saved." *Advocate of Bible Holiness.* Boston: February, 1882.

Pioneer Experiences, or The Gift of Power Received by Faith. New York: W. C. Palmer, Jr., 1868.

Pollock, John Charles. *The Keswick Story: The Authorized History of the Keswick Convention.* London: Hodder and Stoughton, 1964.

Ridgeway, Henry Bascom. *The Life of Rev. Alfred Cookman: with Some Account of His Father, Rev. George Grimston Cookman.* New York: Harper & Brothers, 1874.

Roberts, B. H. *Benjamin Titus Roberts.* North Chili, N.Y.: 1900.

Roberts, B. T., ed. Vol. 2. *The Earnest Christian.* Buffalo, N.Y.: n.d.

Ruth, Christian Wismer. *Entire Sanctification: A Second Blessing.* Chicago: Christian Witness, 1903.

Sangster, W. E. *The Path to Perfection.* New York: Abingdon, 1943.

Schaff, Philip. *History of the Christian Church.* 8 vols. Grand Rapids: Eerdmans, 1960-63.

Simpson, Albert Benjamin. *Wholly Sanctified: with Introduction by Rev. Alfred C. Sneed.* Harrisburg, Pa.: Christian Publications, Inc., 1925.

Smith, Hannah Whitall. *The Christian's Secret of a Happy Life.* Westwood, N.J.: Revell, 1952.

Sperry, W. L. *Those of the Way.* New York: Harper & Bros., 1945.

Steele, Daniel. *Milestone Papers.* New York: Phillips and Hunt, 1876.

Tauler, Johannes. *History and Life of the Reverend Doctor John Tauler of Strasbourg.* London: H. R. Allenson, 1905.

Taylor, Dr. and Mrs. Howard. *Hudson Taylor in Early Years: The Growth of a Soul.* Philadelphia: China Inland Mission, 1912.

Terrill, Joseph Goodwin. *The Life of Rev. John Wesley Redfield.* Titusville, Pa.: Allegheny Wesleyan Methodist, 1889.

Thompson, A. E. *A. B. Simpson: His Life and Work.* Harrisburg, Pa.: Christian Publications, 1960.

Turner, George Allen. *The Vision Which Transforms.* Kansas City: Beacon Hill Press, 1964.

Wach, J. "Caspar Schwenkfeld." *Journal of Religion,* January, 1946, p. 23.

Wesche, P. A. *Henry Clay Morrison, Crusader, Saint.* Herald Press, 1963.

Wesley, John. *The Journal of John Wesley: Popular Edition.* 2 vols. London: C. H. Kelly, 1903.

Williams, W. R. *Me and My House.* Grand Rapids: Eerdmans, 1957.

Wood, John Allen. *Perfect Love: Abridged by John Paul.* Kansas City: Beacon Hill Press, 1944.

———. *Perfect Love: or, Plain Things for Those Who Need Them, Concerning the Doctrine, Experience, Profession and Practice of Christian Holiness.* Chicago: Christian Witness Co., 1910.